GROOMED

GROOMED

Coercion, Control and
a Cold-Blooded Murder

NICOLA TALLANT

First published in the UK in 2025 by Eriu
An imprint of Bonnier Books UK
5th Floor, HYLO, 105 Bunhill Row,
London, EC1Y 8LZ

A CIP catalogue record for this book is available from the British Library.

Trade Paperback ISBN: 978-1-80444-208-1

Also available as an ebook and an audiobook

1 3 5 7 9 10 8 6 4 2

Typeset by IDSUK (Data Connection) Ltd
Printed and bound in Great Britain by Clays Ltd, Elcograf S.p.A.

The authorised representative in the EEA is Bonnier Books
UK (Ireland) Limited.
Registered office address: Floor 3, Block 3, Miesian Plaza,
Dublin 2, D02 Y754, Ireland
compliance@bonnierbooks.ie
www.bonnierbooks.co.uk

"Three may keep a secret, if two of them are dead."
Benjamin Franklin

CONTENTS

PROLOGUE

I'm in a part of the country where I have rarely ventured. The small village of Tynan is located just across the Irish border between the towns of Monaghan in the Republic and Armagh in the North. I would describe it as a hamlet more than a village, although there is a church here, St Vindic's, which stands on a little hillock overlooking the graveyard. There, among the headstones, among the dead, is an epitaph to a young girl taken at the prime of her life. 'In Loving Memory of Katie. A much-loved daughter, sister, granddaughter and aunt. Passed away 9th August 2020. Aged 21 years.' On a little stone butterfly is engraved a memory of a special daughter: 'No tears, no words can ever say how much we love and miss you everyday.' It is a warm August day and it's soon to be Katie Simpson's fourth anniversary. Flowers dance in the breeze and a little rosette sits on the headstone, left by a friend who remembers the happy times she and Katie spent riding horses over jumps and across fields, feeling the freedom blow through their hair. I stand for a moment in the fresh air and look down on the piece of earth where this girl now lies silenced for ever with the secrets of her death. The little cemetery where Katie Simpson is buried overlooks the cottage where she grew up, the place where the stables once stood, where she was drawn, mesmerised, by the beautiful horses she would learn to ride and to trust.

Journalist Tanya Fowles is sitting in my car waiting patiently for me to take in this scene. She often stops by the graveyard to remember the auburn-haired girl whose death has become a crusade of truth and a battle of epic proportions against a system that failed her. She was here the day Katie was buried, lowered into her grave by a man who stole her childhood and her life but who masqueraded as a mourner and a hero. Katie Simpson didn't 'pass away', she was brutally raped and murdered, her death staged as a suicide. That much we now know, thanks to Tanya and a handful of strangers and friends who fought to bring Katie justice in death. Tanya will be my guide, not only today, but throughout this dark story. It's a story that meanders through a world of showjumping and eventing, often regarded as one for the privileged, but which has been rocked by a tale so shocking that it is now only spoken of in whispers.

I'd met Tanya earlier at the shop in Killylea, west of Armagh city, and from there we'd made the short drive to Tynan, chatting as we went. 'Hold up, sorry, pull in,' she suddenly directed me as I realised I'd almost driven right through Tynan. Blink and you'd miss it. An old stone cross dating from the tenth century, which sits in the middle of the village, or the seventeenth-century stone sundial on the graveyard gatepost might draw a historian here, but otherwise there is little to see except the horses.

This is a community that has been steeped in equestrianism for centuries, and in more recent times the Darton Ree stables became the heartbeat of the village. 'It is small but they had the horses,' says Tanya. 'In the mornings people would come out to look at them going out for their exercise in the fields. The jockeys would ride them out and up the road and the locals would come out to see them. And then when the foals would be born the children would want their photographs taken with them. If you lived here you would have been drawn to the stables. A lot of kids helped muck out so they could be near the horses, it was the heart of the village.'

We are parked up on Chapel Hill Road. To our right stands St Vindic's with its stained-glass windows and single tall tower rising to overlook the landscape. Tombstones peep out over the crooked stone wall that surrounds the church. Opposite is a whitewashed village school and the stone cross. There is a row of houses known as Taylor Cottages and across the Abbey Road is the elegant house where Dr Fitz Gillespie ran his surgery and where he started his Darton Ree stables, where champions were bred. The stables are gone and Dr Gillespie is dead, but his children run the business now and have moved it to bigger and more suitable premises some kilometres away.

'I suppose you could say there are two sects here. There are the ones who love horses, ponies, a donkey or whatever stands on four legs and then for others it is trade, a proper business. But what brings everyone together is the horses. There is a dry hunt here that everyone gets involved in but there is no kill. The horses are the backbone of the place,' explains Tanya. It's agricultural land that surrounds us; sheep, beef and dairy. The land is good, and much of it has been owned by the same families for generations.

I start the engine and we begin our tour. 'So you're going to see a stone on the left which will say "Tynan". And believe it or not when you drive through here and pass the church you are through the village, but I am going to take you a different way,' Tanya tells me. 'Take a right turn here . . . And now left.' I steer the car out into the countryside where we can see the fields and the white tape flapping in the wind that marks what was once the race training track. 'It was a really long track and good for getting the animals fit, but it's disused now because they've moved to other ground.'

I've driven around now a few times, out into the countryside and the rolling green fields and back through the village, but I'm confused. 'Tanya, where is the shop?' I ask. She laughs and points out the single pharmacy, the only business in the town. 'There is a bus,' she says. 'One in the morning, one in the afternoon and occasionally one at night.' I grew up in Dublin, a city spread that now houses two million people, small by European standards but quite a bit larger than Tynan. 'So you'd be totally trapped here, then,' I declare, and Tanya laughs.

The border with the south is just minutes away. In fact, ten minutes' drive south-west would take you to Glaslough, a village in County Monaghan dominated by the beautiful Castle Leslie, a former stately home now painstakingly restored to a luxury hotel, a favourite of celebrities and the well-heeled. As we drive we see a dog lying on the side of the road and Tanya tells me to pull in. 'Is he okay? He's not injured, is he?' The dog, a border collie, is only playing dead. He observes us for an instant and then bolts off. 'Honestly, you wouldn't believe what I have brought home, I came in with a raven one day and my husband just said "Where the hell are you gonna put that?"' I can see which of the 'sects' Tanya is in. She loves horses and is a competent rider. In fact, she loves all animals and, she tells me, she is the proud mother of a number of very demanding cats. 'That's it, by the way,' says Tanya. 'There's nothing else to show you here, that is the extent of it. Believe it or not, Nicola, you've just finished with Tynan. So now I'll take you back to Caledon. We'll loop around.'

As we drive she starts talking about 'Johnny'. He was only about 19 when he came to work in Tynan, moving into a house in Caledon, where he got state aid with the rent. 'I think what brought him here was Jill. As far as I know she was already working for Dr Gillespie. She was a jockey. Nobody knew much about Johnny's background then, just that he was from Derry and there was a story about his father, that he was rich, but that he didn't really know him. He'd been raised by his grandparents and it seemed that he was very spoiled. A lot of people thought he was good-looking, although I never did. He'd big rosy cheeks and floppy hair but the younger girls reckoned he was gorgeous and he loved that.'

As we leave Tynan and head for the Coolkill Road to Caledon, we look at some newly built houses. 'Just while I remember, that is where the barn was. See, nothing is ever in all the one ground here, you have to cross roads and walk a bit. That was all sold off and developed, but that was the barn and at two o'clock every day Johnny used to disappear into the barn. Now you see the wee sign there . . . go down Abbey Road and head on to Caledon.'

Fields fly past me on both sides, vast open landscapes where cattle and sheep graze. In the back Tanya is condensing this story into a confusing mass of names and events. There is Abi Lyle and Hayley Robb, Jill Robinson and Christina Simpson. Then there is Paul Lusby, but we will get to all that later. There are people from this place, whose names we will protect, who didn't like Johnny or his ways. There is the young boy, Aaron McWilliams, who used to follow him around like a puppy. And then there is Katie, the reason I am here.

'I'll show you where he lived in Caledon. And I'll show you where that thing happened with Abi,' says Tanya. 'He took her there after he took her over the border. This is where she was rescued. The house was always known as the "jockey house" because the man who owned it rented it out to them and they would be working in the surrounding area. He met Abi at a showjumping contest and got her number.'

We arrive in Caledon, a bigger village with a big wide market street. It's dominated by the large house where the Alexander family still live. 'Everywhere here is either owned or leased by the Caledon estate. The earl is the big employer, but he doesn't be about that much. There are pretty stone houses that were built by the estate but they've been sold on mostly. A lot of people were born in the estate grounds in the past, their parents were labourers and after a wee while they'd buy a bit of land or they'd be gifted a bit and they'd build something. Then there are new developments. Johnny lived in Chestnut Manor,' says Tanya. We find the house. It's in the corner of a small development; stone clad and end of terrace.

'That is where he threatened to put her in a bath of bleach. He took her shoes and everything,' says Tanya. 'But after he went to jail he came back here and Christina was waiting for him. She and Jill supported him all the way through that and they all had a big party for him when he got out of jail. It was incredible the way that happened. It was like a cult that he had built up around himself and he was so young.'

The road will take us further from here, across the border to Donegal and to the stately Port Hall, north to Derry, and into a very dark world where a young man with rosy cheeks developed a power over women that would end in a tangled knot of murder and betrayal.

This is no story of gangland crime, where money motivates most and where death is simply another way of doing business. This will be a far more complex dive into the human soul and its depravities than the underworld ever throws up. For me this journey began just two months before, in a courtroom in Derry where three ordinary-looking women – Jill Robinson, Hayley Robb and Rose De Montmorency Wright – stood for sentencing, convicted of a betrayal of epic proportions. The Crown Court had heard that the case centred on the murder of 21-year-old showjumper Katie Simpson, who had died at the hands of Jonathan Creswell, who had raped her prior to her murder. But by the time the women stood in the dock Creswell himself was dead by suicide, and they had been left to carry the can:

Particularly pertinent to the sentencing exercise this court must now embark upon, he and others made efforts to cover up what he had done in the prelude to her death. Creswell tried to make her death look like a suicide. Together with others, he disposed of and interfered with evidence with the inevitable consequence of misleading those investigating her death. Accounts were provided by Creswell and these Defendants which were intended to and had the effect of protecting him from being suspected of or having a role in her death. Mr Creswell himself created a fiction, pretending to others he had found Katie, hanging in a stairwell from a strap, claiming she had taken her own life. These Defendants did not know the truth about how she had met her death. However, they ascribed to and were complicit in his conspiracy of silence.

Robb faced three indictments: one of withholding information and two counts of perverting the course of justice. Robinson was to be sentenced for perverting the course of justice, and De Montmorency Wright for withholding information. All three were friends of Katie Simpson and her older sister, Christina, who had been in a long-term relationship with Jonathan Creswell and was the mother of his two children. While prosecutors had at one point considered charging Christina, she had not been brought before the court.

All three women were given suspended sentences for their roles in the cover-up, and as they walked free from court, their heads bowed, family members waited to drive them away from the waiting media. But far from being over, the story of what happened to Katie Simpson had really just begun.

CHAPTER 1

THE BIG HOUSES

The small villages of Tynan in County Armagh, Caledon in County Tyrone and Glaslough in County Monaghan are separated by three county borders but just a few miles of road. Nestled north-east of Monaghan town and south-west of Belfast, they are surrounded by rolling grasslands and mature forests. Sheep and cattle farming is commonplace, and one of the largest herds of red deer in Ireland have bred there. Hedgerows introduced by English landlords in the 1800s to create boundaries between their tenant holdings dot the landscapes and in May they are white with hawthorn blossom. Woodlands mark the seasons with their carpets of snowdrops, wild garlic and bluebells. Churches, Catholic, Presbyterian and Church of Ireland, stand on high points in the villages, while stone-built houses line the wide main streets.

All three areas are steeped in reminders of stark times in the history of Ireland: British imperialism, famine and the peerage of the country directed by English monarchs. South of the border, the Castle Leslie estate, which dominates the tiny village of Glaslough, with its population of 350, has been in the Leslie family since 1665. Handed down over four centuries, it is now run as a hotel by Samantha Leslie, who inherited it from her father, Desmond, a Spitfire pilot who would later document his belief in UFOs in his book *Flying Saucers Have Landed*. Awash with stories of ancient politics, grand parties and ghosts, it was home to the many colourful characters of the Leslie family who passed the estate down through chains of siblings and children.

The Leslie family trace their ancestry all the way back to Attila the Hun, the ruthless and barbaric Hungarian known for his military feats and credited as being the final destroyer of the Roman Empire. The first Leslie to come to Ireland was Bishop John, who in the 1600s built Raphoe Castle in County Donegal, defeated Cromwell's forces, married at the age of 67 and bought Castle Leslie, where he died aged 100. Throughout the eighteenth century and into the nineteenth, descendant after descendant took on the estate and developed it. During the famine a soup kitchen fed the starving. Fine furniture, art and ornaments were collected and passed down to the next custodians while the vast family wealth eventually went south in a badly advised investment in Russian Railway Bonds. By the 1960s the estate was in the hands of the eccentric Desmond, who tried to turn it into a viable business, opening a nightclub, Annabel's on the Bog, in the rural backwater. A successful writer, he married twice, had six children, produced films and music, opened an equestrian centre and finally retired to France. Undoubtedly his business plans for his ancestral home and estate were thwarted by the Troubles over the border in Northern Ireland and the threat posed by IRA terrorists to those who lived in the 'big houses'.

By 1991 the estate and the vast expense of running it fell to the hands of Sammy, a child of her father's second marriage, who became its trustee in her early 20s, and who was keen to follow

Desmond's efforts to make it commercially viable and to keep it in the family. She set about returning it to its former glory and opening it to the public.

Tea rooms funded a new roof for the old conservatory, guestrooms opened and houses and buildings were sold while the castle was slowly returned to the showstopper it once was with the help of EU cross-border funding. In 2001 Desmond died, aged 79, and while described in various obituaries as an eccentric and a spiritualist he was also noted as being among the first Anglo-Irish big house guardians to try to turn his birthright into a viable business. By 2002, his daughter had begun to realise his dream when the estate hit world headlines as the venue for the marriage of former Beatle Paul McCartney and the model Heather Mills. For days, the media camped outside the gates of the castle, hoping to catch a glimpse of the couple and to be sure that the wedding was actually going ahead. In the event the star of the show was not the superstar or his bride but the madcap Sir John Leslie, an octogenarian disco dancer affectionately known as Uncle Jack, who slipped out the front of the castle dressed in a kilt and whispered to the world's press: 'They're getting married on Tuesday, but it's a secret.'

After the celebrity nuptials the reputation and facilities of Castle Leslie continued to grow as it was transformed into a hospitality powerhouse; a venue for weddings, romantic weekends and activity holidays. Sammy Leslie continued to live there while working full time to keep it running and develop its stables, fisheries and guest accommodation. Until he died in 2016 at the age of 99, Uncle Jack mingled with guests, eating in the dining hall and telling those who would listen about his regular trips to Ibiza to party at Privilege, one of the world's biggest nightclubs.

North of Glaslough and just six kilometres away, another of Ireland's 'big houses' had a far darker history. Tynan in County Armagh, a village with a population of just 71 at the 2011 census, was dominated for centuries by the huge Gothic Tynan Abbey, built in 1750 by the Stronge family and surrounded at one point by an estate of over 8,000 acres. By 1923, as vast estates like the Abbey came under attack for the first time, the family offered safe accommodation at the mansion to the British police force, the Royal Ulster Constabulary. Later, during the Second World War, it housed British, Belgian and American troops. However, the generosity that had worked as private security for the occupants during the War of Independence was not in place during the Troubles, and 21 January 1981 would mark one of the most violent attacks on the aristocracy in the history of modern Ireland.

By then the war was raging in Northern Ireland, where the Provisional Irish Republican Army sought an end to British rule through a campaign of violence. The Provos, as they were known, had emerged in 1969 following a split in the original IRA and the broader Irish republican movement and within three years had become the dominant faction. The Troubles had begun in 1970 following violence at civil rights marches. With support and funding from the Palestine Liberation Organization and the Libyan leader Muammar Gaddafi, the Provos took on the Empire. A bombing campaign resulted in internment, which united Catholics in opposition to the government, adding fuel to the flames. Tensions increased further after Bloody Sunday in Derry, in January 1972, when the British Army killed 14 unarmed civilians attending a civil rights march. By 1973 the Provos had taken their bombing campaign to London and to Birmingham, where 21 people were killed in pub bombings. Throughout the rest of the decade the Troubles turned Northern Ireland into a war zone as loyalist and republican paramilitaries carried out atrocities, bombings and assassinations. Belfast and Derry, the two largest cities, bore the brunt of the killings and became ripe recruitment grounds for young men on both sides of the divide. But the border counties too had built up violent brigades and were hugely active in both the fight and the smuggling that helped fund it. One of the most dangerous groupings was the South Armagh Brigade. In 1974 the then Northern Ireland secretary, Merlyn Rees, christened the area 'Bandit Country'. The East Tyrone Brigade of the Provos also had a reputation for savagery and were known as one of the most active paramilitary groups during the Troubles. No-go zones for the British Army and the RUC were created as the units pushed to expand their territory through murder and fear.

The Stronge family had lived at Tynan Abbey since 1711 and the vast property had been passed down through successive clergymen, merchants, landlords and staunch Unionist politicians, many Oxford- and Eton-educated. Like the Leslie family, the Stronges hosted parties, collected fine art and furniture and lived and died in splendour. In the mid-1800s Sir James Stronge, 3rd Baronet, established the Tynan Hunt, which later merged into the Tynan and Armagh Harriers. By 1939 Tynan Abbey had been passed to the 8th Baronet, Sir Norman Stronge, a war hero who had fought at the Battle of the Somme before becoming an Ulster Unionist MP and, later, Speaker of the Northern House of Commons. He was also a prominent member of the Orange Order and leading member of the Church of Ireland and until his death regularly served as rector of Tynan parish church.

By 1981, Sir Norman was 86 and living at Tynan Abbey with his only son, James, in their huge property surrounded by 800 remaining acres of land. On the night of 21 January they were in the library, one of the few rooms they used. Up to 14 IRA men, later described as some of the most hardened Republicans from Armagh and Tyrone, arrived at the property and blew in the front door with a grenade. Sir Norman managed to let off a flare, but the IRA shot at the RUC men who arrived to help. A second police team was sent in, but by the time they got there, fires had been started in various parts of the house, and firefighters were called in. When first responders from Portadown eventually got into the house they found Sir Norman and James dead from gunshot wounds. The IRA issued a statement saying: 'This deliberate attack on the symbols of hated unionism was a direct reprisal for a whole series of loyalist assassinations and murder attacks on the nationalist peoples and nationalist activities.' The terrorists had destroyed the Abbey, leaving only a shell of the building and ending eight generations of the family's occupation of it. By 1998 the ruins of the building were demolished and the site levelled, leaving just the arch of the front door surround, while the land remained in the possession of Sir Norman's eldest daughter, Mrs Daphne Marian Kingan, until her death in 2002, when it was passed down to her son, James Kingan. On the fortieth anniversary of Sir Norman and James's deaths, Kingan told the BBC's *Good Morning Ulster* programme: 'They were armed with submachine guns, grenades. They blew in the front door and found my grandfather and my uncle in the library. My grandfather was 86 and quite deaf, so always had the television on full volume.' Kingan had been at his grandfather's funeral at Tynan, which was attended by hundreds of people from across Northern Ireland and Britain from lords, politicians, church leaders to ordinary local people.

Just three kilometres north of Tynan Abbey, in Caledon, County Tyrone, the Alexander family had owned their vast estate since 1775, when James Alexander purchased it for the equivalent of €15 million in today's money. He had made his fortune in the East India Company, a stock company formed to trade with Asia across the Indian Ocean. The company was at its peak during Alexander's time, accounting for half the world's trade in commodities like salt, spice and silk, and it went on to rule large swathes of Pakistan and India. James Alexander built Caledon House, becoming Baron Caledon, then Viscount and finally, in 1800, the 1st Earl of Caledon. Under the 2nd Earl the village was created, with more than two hundred stone houses and a school for Catholic and Protestant girls. Just like the Leslie estate and Tynan Abbey, Caledon was passed on through generations of family members over more than two hundred years and is currently the home of the 7th Earl, Nicholas Alexander, and his wife, Lady Amanda Caledon. The Caledon estate was also targeted by the IRA during the Troubles, although no such atrocities like those at Tynan Abbey occurred. In 1972 a bomb caused extensive damage to the property and a year later two bombs were discovered on monuments in the grounds. In 1991 a Provisional IRA unit targeted it again, spraying it with assault rifles. An IRA statement released afterwards claimed that the unit involved had fired over 700 rounds and that the British soldiers guarding it were the intended target, not the family in the house.

The privileged living in the 'big houses' of Ireland had been dwindling in number for decades. Since the beginning of the twentieth century, deep-seated political unrest coupled with anxieties around their tenuous financial future in the modern world, has seen many lock up their doors for good. The financial incentives offered under the Land Act of 1903 meant that many landlords sold up their piles and left their estates and farmland. Those who remained found themselves in ever smaller numbers in a fast-changing society. By the beginning of the twentieth century just 1,500 large estates remained in the hands of the gentry across the country. Fewer numbers meant more exposure to the growing movement against the unfair land purchase and peerage practices of the past. The first wave of the destruction of these houses came during the War of Independence, when they were identified as a powerful symbol of British colonialism and imperialism. In 1920 many houses were burned because their owners were seen as sympathetic to the Crown and because of long-held grudges that the lands had been purchased unfairly in the first place. During the Civil War of 1922, as the Crown forces withdrew, republicans started to torch what they saw as symbols of colonialism; Artramon House in Wexford, Ballycarty House in Tralee, County Kerry and Cavananore in County Louth were just some of those demolished. In the North, too, homes were targeted and looted, among them Antrim Castle and Roxborough Castle in County Tyrone. After the 1923 Land Act was passed, the Irish Land Commission redistributed thousands of acres and acquired under compulsory order many of the houses that had been damaged by fire. It also inherited many empty and abandoned estates, most of which were then demolished.

The growing sense of isolation amongst the landed classes meant they often stuck together and the proximity of Glaslough,

Tynan and Caledon meant that the offspring and the wider families living there at any given time socialised together and even shared staff. Not only did their presence, as the heartbeat of their local villages, mean that they were steeped in the history of wars and great political dynasties, but they also brought to the small communities a love of horses and all things equine, creating employment and attracting outsiders to the opportunities they saw there.

From the mid-1800s, when the Dublin Horse Show was established, becoming one of the most important events on the landed gentry's summer circuit, everything changed. Throughout the 1900s, horse racing, showjumping and even horse breeding became more populist and a series of Irish government initiatives turned what had been an elitist hobby into one of Ireland's most important and inclusive industries. In 1968, as Minister for Finance, Charlie Haughey, a keen horseman himself, introduced a tax exemption for stallion fees in the Finance Act. In response, some of the most famous breeders and richest owners from across the world, like Sheikh Mohammed bin Rashid Al Maktoum and the Aga Khan, bought up stud farms, while their racehorses took to the tracks with IRE on their backs. Coolmore Stud, under John Magnier, grew and became recognised as one of the best in the world. In the Dáil in the 1970s Haughey said, 'Bloodstock breeding provides first class employment in many areas where it would be impossible to provide employment of a similar calibre in any other way.'

The end of the Troubles was a welcome boost to a thriving sector. The economies on both sides of the border began to grow and so too did job opportunities for many. In the early 2000s Liam Connellan, the former President of the RDS, produced a report setting out the principles for a new organisation to represent all 32 counties as a governing body for all equestrian sport. The backbone of the report was that all disciplines, from dressage to racing, should come under the one body, which was eventually set up as Horse Sport Ireland in 2006. Within the next decade the massive industry would be valued at more than €800 million to the Irish economy and provide over 14,000 jobs, largely in rural Ireland; and it was projected to continue to grow.

CHAPTER 2

GOLDEN-HAIRED BOY

By the time he rode into Tynan village, Johnny Creswell was exactly the type of young man Horse Sport Ireland, the semi-state body set up to develop Ireland's booming equestrian industry, would identify as a career equestrian. From Derry, he had been immersed in the industry from an early age, was uninterested in school and had dropped out of education. His ambition was to work full time in the yards and stables where he had spent his childhood. He wanted to first apprentice as a jockey and then make the trajectory into trainer and owner, ultimately eyeing up his own stables and stud. His timing was excellent; what would have once been seen as a dead-end job as a farmhand had become a role brimming with promise in an industry on a gold rush.

Horse Sport Ireland had just been established with the aim of growing equestrian sport and promoting Ireland internationally as a place for horse breeding, leisure horse-riding and training. Horse Racing Ireland had reported growth for consecutive years and 2006 was a record year at the race tracks: 1.4 million people had attended racing events, despite competition from the World Cup and Ryder Cup and 15 cancelled meetings due to bad weather. Additionally, Ireland had celebrated ten winners at Cheltenham, including the prestigious Gold Cup, the Champion Hurdle and the Champion Chase. In his Fact Book that year, Brian Kavanagh, Chief Executive of Horse Racing Ireland, reported a 31 per cent growth in bloodstock sales at public auction (€191 million), a 10 per cent growth in on-course betting (€262 million) and a growth of 5 per cent in prize money (€55 million). 'There is a broad consensus that the current prize money levels have helped to encourage owners and trainers to buy the best horses, keep them in training in Ireland and compete in the top races at home and abroad. This in turn provides employment throughout the regions and helps us to retain and build an unequalled equine skills base,' Kavanagh said.

Creswell's route to his first apprenticeship at Darton Ree yard in the heart of Tynan village was a typical one for many young jockeys. He had horses in his blood and from an early age had been riding ponies and competing in showjumping events. While he was not a natural in the saddle he had the determination to hang on for dear life no matter what the terrain or speed. That had made him an excellent huntsman and well-regarded showjumper, but neither would pay the bills. To take his first tentative steps to a proper career he needed to apprentice so that he could race point-to-points across Ireland in the major and smaller events that were staged every week.

Born to a single mother in January 1988, he had started life in a city fraught with tension and violence. His birth came just days before a planned march to remember the Bloody Sunday atrocity, which had left an indelible mark on his native Derry. Even 16 years on from the horrors of the ill-fated civil rights march, RUC patrols and blocks surrounded Derry in the run-up to the planned remembrance marches, and security was tight. Donna Creswell was still only a teenager when she made her way through the chaos to Altnagelvin Hospital to give birth to what would be her only child.

There were stories around Donna's pregnancy and whispers about her liaison with Herbie Lusby, a wealthy landowner for whom she had been working as a farm labourer on his vast property outside the town. Lusby was married with a young son and daughter and the announcement of the pregnancy had caused some tension in both homes, but the arrival of the baby had quelled that, particularly at Donna's, where he was doted on in a house full of adults and where his grandparents James and Sandra stepped in to help rear him, while his uncles and aunt, Alan, Gordon, Richard and Caroline, were on hand to help Donna get back on her feet.

Tensions were high in Northern Ireland and in the months after his birth the news was dominated by high-profile events, including the killing of the Gibraltar Three, Daniel McCann, Seán Savage and Mairéad Farrell, by the SAS. In March at Milltown Cemetery, at the funeral of the three, loyalist Michael Stone used pistols and grenades to attack mourners, killing three people and wounding 60. Much of the attack was filmed by TV cameras. Days later, at the funeral of Kevin Brady, one of the three shot by Stone, two British Army corporals were surrounded and later shot dead after driving a car into the funeral procession. By May the Provisional IRA had taken their fight to the Netherlands, where three members of the Royal Air Force were killed. A month later six off-duty soldiers died when an IRA bomb exploded their van. Later that month a helicopter was shot from the sky in

Armagh by a unit of the South Armagh Brigade. On the political stage the ongoing targeting of British security personnel had led to a huge clash between the Irish Taoiseach Charles Haughey and British Prime Minister Margaret Thatcher, who accused the Gardaí of being less than professional while the IRA plotted atrocities in the Republic. During a heated meeting Thatcher had warned Haughey that her one objective was to 'beat the IRA': 'I will never be prepared to walk out and let the terrorists win.' Later that year marked the twentieth anniversary of the 1968 civil rights march. Among those that took part in the memorial march were leading Sinn Féin officials Gerry Adams and Martin McGuinness. Security along the route of the march was tight but the RUC prevented loyalists planning a counter-demonstration. The outspoken Democratic Unionist Party leader, Reverend Ian Paisley, who had travelled to Derry with many of his supporters, was involved in angry exchanges and he claimed he was pushed from a police Land Rover as he tried to wave a Union Jack.

At home the Creswell family had a lot to be thankful for. Outside was undoubtedly a strange and dangerous place but inside the house, baby Johnny, with his blond hair and rosy cheeks, had brought the family a sense of joy in stark contrast to the constant grim narrative of day-to-day life. As he grew, the atrocities continued across Armagh, Fermanagh, Down and Tyrone, but in 1993, when he was just five, the war took a shocking turn and the violence came frighteningly close to home. In October the UDA (the Ulster Defence Association), using the cover name Ulster Freedom Fighters, claimed responsibility for a gun attack on the Rising Sun bar in Greysteel in which eight civilians were killed and 12 wounded. In a country in the grip of a war, when murders were commonplace the attack stood out for the crass shouts of one gunman, who yelled 'trick or treat' before spraying the crowded room, a reference to a Halloween party that was taking place. The UFF would claim that the horror shootings were in revenge for the Shankill Road bombing days earlier, when nine people were killed when an IRA bomb exploded prematurely at a fish shop. People lived in fear and every day more were traumatised by the history playing out on their streets.

In the yards and the stables surrounding Derry there was a sense of distance from the terrorism and Donna was keen to introduce her child to horses as soon as she could. While chaos and upheaval was never far away, where the wealthy gathered it seemed life was almost untouched by the violence and rioting that engulfed the vast estates of Derry like Creggan and the Bogside. As soon as he was old enough, Donna enrolled Johnny at the pony club at Eglinton Equestrian Club in Derry, where he quickly took to the sport. A lively and boisterous boy, he showed no fear of the ponies or bigger horses that trotted about the large yards and arenas. At weekends he'd be schooled in riding and jumping, and he often went with his mother to muck out or feed the horses after school and during long summer holidays. Peace was finally on the horizon and there was a sense of opportunity in the air. By the time the Good Friday Agreement was signed on 10 April 1998, Johnny was ten years old and well on his way to being one of Northern Ireland's success stories, a child born into the worst of the Troubles but one looking at a far more stable and secure future. In fact, he was so good at handling a pony that he was hand-picked by Aldyth Roulston to ride her champions, which regularly competed at Showjumping Ireland events.

Aldyth was extremely successful at breeding ponies but she had no children herself. Many people believed that young Johnny was her own son, she doted on him so much and he spent so much time with her, travelling and performing in the RDS and other venues. Aldyth, many said, 'had him ruined'. He had learned from the best and had enjoyed the best of everything available to a rider from such a young age; the most expensive tack and riding gear, the best ponies and first-class transport and stabling. The relationship eventually turned sour when Aldyth and Donna fell out, but by that point Creswell was already a name in showjumping circles and was about to move on to eventing.

While Johnny was prospering in the saddle, schooling had evaded him. He was not good at reading or writing and struggled to keep up in the classroom. Although his father had not been a steady presence in his life, Herbie Lusby had kept a watching eye over his love child and had helped out financially and encouraged him in his love of riding. Lusby was unconventional in every way, but he was known as a decent and generous man. He was 40 years old when his brief affair with Donna led to her pregnancy, but he'd weathered the gossip and tried to keep his own family together. Lusby was from a large family and he'd been born and bred on the land. His father, Noel, had worked hard for success after inheriting from his own father, Herbert, a smallholding of 20 acres on which he grazed 20 cattle on the Waterside in Derry. The story went that the Lusbys were from wealthy Catholic stock who'd been pillaged and run out of England and who had come to Derry to start again.

Noel was hardworking and doubled his farm to 40 acres, later, along with his wife Anne, extending it to an impressive 340 acres.

Along with their nine children they travelled the country to attend shows, including the RDS agriculture event in Ballsbridge in Dublin, where they displayed their livestock. It was the Ayrshire breed that brought Noel to prominence, but he turned his skills to the French Limousin, large beef cattle with a bright tan coat. He knew the importance of representative bodies and funding and would eventually become Chair of the Northern Ireland Cattle Club. Many of the Lusby children had followed Noel into farming, including Herbie, who'd developed an interest in breeding himself, in particular Appaloosa ponies. He was farming at a time when British soldiers often hid, camouflaged and armed, around his land near Beragh Hill. He was known to have no time for them or for British occupation and he supported Catholic youth schemes as community leaders tried to teach them skills and trades.

Herbie Lusby had been very well placed when developers came calling with an offer for his land. The entire development and growth of Derry had been controlled by a gerrymandered council since his own father Noel farmed the land, building up a huge cattle herd, which had given Herbie a decent start in life. His own lands were located beside the old US military camp known as Springtown, which had been central to the rise of the civil rights movement. In the 1940s poor Catholic families, desperate for a roof over their heads, had broken into the old camp and taken up residence in the tin huts. For years the Unionist-controlled city council had charged them rent and promised them they would be housed in proper homes in the city. But the housing never materialised and conditions deteriorated as the council feared that moving Catholics to other areas would affect their votes in local elections. When the residents eventually took their demands in a silent protest to Derry's Guildhall the council was forced to move them, an event which in turn led to the establishment of the Northern Ireland Civil Rights Association. The Springtime families were largely rehoused in the huge Creggan estate, built in the 1950s. But the Unionist council made sure that the Catholics were corralled together into one electoral ward, which included Creggan, the Bogside and the Brandywell districts, so that they couldn't get a foothold in local politics. As the population grew, the huge Catholic area of the Creggan spread northwards towards a housing estate known as the Glen, which had been mainly allocated to the families of RUC officers and the notorious B Specials, who began to move out. When the Troubles erupted in 1969, the outflow of the Protestant population continued, becoming a flood after Bloody Sunday. As the Troubles continued throughout the 1970s the Catholic population continued to spread northwards, edging ever closer to the significant holding of land owned by Lusby. By the 1980s the old Londonderry Council had been renamed Derry City Council and there were significant numbers of Catholics in well-paid employment in big companies. Derry also had a second generation of university-educated professionals, including teachers, and a growing middle class who wanted out of the Creggan and Bogside areas but who were still uncomfortable about taking up residence in the Protestant Waterside area. There was still more than a decade of the low-intensity conflict to run until the Provisional IRA ceasefire was called in August 1994, so land on the city's west bank became much sought after. Lusby had cashed in his chips to developers who had planned and were set to build hundreds of new semi-detached and detached houses and bungalows on what had been his farm. The development would become known as the Foyle Springs housing estates.

At the same time a rare property came up for sale near the shores of the River Foyle on the Donegal/Tyrone border. Lusby snapped it up, seeing it as the ideal location to build a new business around horses. Port Hall was a stunning old country house built in the mid-1700s and described on the Buildings of Ireland website as an 'impressive and sophisticated small-scale Palladian country house . . . arguably the finest building of its type and date in Donegal.' Port Hall had history. Just like Castle Leslie, Tynan Abbey and Caledon Estate, it was a throwback to a time of colonialism when the rich and privileged few lived in big houses. Port Hall had been built for Judge John Vaughan, who served as a Grand Juror to Donegal, and it remained in his family until 1791, at which point it was let out. During the nineteenth century it was in the ownership of the Clarke family, who held 273 acres at the site. A British lawyer, Anthony Marreco, owned it from the 1950s until the 1980s. He was involved in the trials of former Nazis at Nuremberg and was a founding member of Amnesty International. He carefully repaired and renovated the house during his time there.

By the time Lusby moved to Donegal he was intent on creating a viable business that he could hand down to his eldest son, Daniel. Together they set about developing Port Hall into a prestigious stud farm with varied equestrian offerings such as pony club classes and breeding and training facilities. But he'd also kept in touch with Donna and with his son's blossoming career; Jonathan had chosen an expensive sport. By 2001, when he was 13, Creswell was riding at Lenamore Stables in Muff, County Donegal, regularly placing first and clearing rounds. Lenamore, on the border of Donegal and Derry, was one of the most impressive equestrian centres in the area. It had been developed by Geraldine Graham, who had turned her father's dairy farm into a riding school, livery yard and breeding centre. In June of that year, he placed first six times, in Limavady, Lenamore Stables and at AJS Promotions events. His record continued throughout the year and, that August, he placed first at the National Pony and Yearling Championships. In October he placed sixth at Cavan Equestrian Centre south of the border and in November he retired in the first round but at all other events he was highly successful. In 2002 Donna was listed as the owner of Sparkling Rossnashane, a bay mare, with her son listed as the jockey. Over the course of that year his record continued and he placed first at a National Pony and Young Rider Championships.

By 2003 Johnny had dropped out of school and was riding almost full time on Geraldine Graham's Lenamore Lady Luck, placing first 15 times throughout Derry and Donegal shows, and also on Lenamore De Ja Vu. Although he was only 15 years old Johnny brimmed with alpha male confidence, both in and out of the saddle. In the yard he was assertive and dominated conversations, often rough-housing with the other stable hands. He'd also developed a crude narrative when it came to women and often made inappropriate remarks to them, but his self-assured demeanour made him appear older than his years and he also knew exactly how to turn on the charm.

Despite being older by eight years, jockey Jill Robinson found herself drawn to the teenage horseman in a way that astounded both her and those who knew her. Robinson was well respected in the industry and highly sought after by trainers and owners for her skills. She came from Omagh in County Tyrone and was a key organiser of the town's Annual Agricultural and Horse Show. She was also active in the Tyrone Farming Society and known for her organisational and administrative skills as well as her equestrian abilities. She was pretty, too; blonde, with sparkling blue eyes, and an athletic figure honed by years in the saddle. While she could have had her pick of men, Robinson was enthralled by the teenager with the ruddy cheeks, and by the time he turned 16 the pair were an item.

Neither Johnny nor Jill cared what people said about them and the significant age gap between them, and they made no secret of the fact that they were in a romantic relationship. While the natural order would suggest that, given her maturity, Jill should have held the balance of power in the relationship, it was Johnny who was regularly heard chastising her, often in front of their peers, while he continued to make waves on horseback as he confidently improved his form. In 2005 he was ranked in the Youth Continental Regional Championships at Saumur in France on the horse Nees Reven. He rode Ballydown at Necarne Castle and again at Tattersalls in 2006. That same year, aged 18, he was named as the third reserve on Ireland's Junior European Championships team – the closest he would ever get to international sporting fame. Like many keen horsemen, showjumping had been Johnny's first love and it was through eventing and the social life that went with it that he had made connections and gained an understanding of the business. He'd travelled throughout Northern Ireland and across the border for almost a decade competing over jumps. But when he rode his first point-to-point at Tyrella, County Down a year later he got hooked on the speed and the sheer rush of the race. Point-to-point had emerged in the late 1800s as hunts in both Ireland and England organised their own race meetings and steeplechasing became more popular. By now, it was seen as a starting point for young jockeys like Johnny who dreamed of glory at Cheltenham, Aintree or Galway and who realised that there was no money in showjumping.

Those who knew where Johnny's true skills lay when it came to horse riding could see why point-to-point, high-speed races over jumps, would suit him. He was not an elegant rider and sat awkwardly on a horse, but he could hold on no matter what was thrown at him. He was brave and got a kick out of the speed and the thunder of the race. Injuries from falls were often career-ending for jockeys, but Johnny's habit of hanging on no matter what would stand to him. A career as a jockey meant two things: Johnny needed an apprenticeship and a reputable yard to work at; and he also needed to keep his weight down to under nine stone, something that would require discipline and self-control, early mornings, long days and late nights. He started to look for opportunities and when his on–off girlfriend Jill Robinson told him there was an opening at a stables in Armagh he jumped at the chance of getting out of Derry and the family home and moving full time to the village of Tynan in 2008. Jill was a hard worker and had impressed the Gillespie family, who owned the stables. They knew that any jockey she recommended would be good for their business and an asset to the stables. Jill was already an accomplished and busy jockey and at Tynan was hoping to get experience in breeding and training. For Creswell the calibre of horses at Tynan was a big draw, but he hoped that there would also be plenty of extra work in the nearby estates of Caledon and Castle Leslie, where there were still horses that needed to be exercised and where casual work would supplement his income.

Darton Ree Stables in Tynan was established by Dr Fitz Gillespie at the back of his medical practice, which for decades had served the village and the surrounding areas. The horse-mad doctor lived in a sprawling whitewashed house directly opposite Tynan church, where Sir Norman Stronge had preached before his terrible death, and for years he'd treated patients in one of his living rooms. Dr Gillespie's own father had run the Tynan surgery, and Fitz, short for Fitzroy, had attended Trinity College Dublin, where he'd met his wife Barbara, also a doctor. The couple returned to Tynan in 1964, after old Dr Gillespie's death, and together worked and raised their three children, Gael, Patrick and Rollo. Thirty years after their return the couple moved the practice from their home to premises at the newly renovated village school. When he wasn't attending the sick or elderly, Dr Gillespie loved nothing better than to spend time with his horses. He bought land and built stables and started to breed horses in his spare time. By 1971 his horse Duplate won the local fixture at Farmacaffley. Fitz, as he was known outside the surgery, was an avid huntsman and with his status in the community became the chairman of the Tynan and Armagh Hunt, established hundreds of years before by the Stronge family. He became a senior member of the Turf Club of Ireland and by 1992 was celebrating when his horse Repeat The Dose, which he'd bred at Tynan, won the Cathcart Chase at the famous Cheltenham Festival. Other horses sired at his yard included Blue Alliance and Bahia De Palma. When his children came of age they all became involved in the growing business.

But it wasn't just the Gillespies who were proud of the horses and their achievements. The whole village adored them and many came out to watch in the mornings as the riders and horses paraded through the streets before making their way to the fields for exercise. In a way the riders were looked up to as much as the horses, idolised like rock stars. And when the handsome Johnny came to town he made many young female hearts flutter.

CHAPTER 3

BIG FISH, SMALL POND

Johnny Creswell loved the idea of being a big fish in a small pond and it didn't take him long to settle into Darton Ree, where he felt the status of his new position. Brimming with confidence and charisma, he took on the swagger of the handsome horseman he believed himself to be. While moving to a tiny village like Tynan, with its one shop, would be a culture shock for many young city folk, Johnny had been immersed in the life of horses since he was a small child and was used to the rough and ready lifestyle; mucking out, working in all weather and the constant travel that went with it.

At Darton Ree he and Jill were soon running the show and when they weren't riding out or taking on chores at the yard, Johnny loved to mingle with the visitors, particularly the women who brought their young daughters to learn to ride horses. He seemed to enthral and mesmerise women of all ages and at the stables he was regularly surrounded by young girls who vied for his attention. He was attentive to their parents, showering compliments on them about the abilities of their daughters. He was tough but charming and his impulsive personality and larger-than-life presence made him someone who people wanted to be close to.

Creswell rented a house at nearby Caledon, just over the border into County Tyrone, at the Chestnut Manor estate located behind some of the stone-built homes constructed by the Alexander family hundreds of years before. He qualified for a housing grant as his salary was low, but like other jockeys at the Darton Ree Stables, he topped it up by riding for the local gentry.

Lady Jane Alexander had come to live in a property outside the estate of her brother, Lord Caledon, right in the heart of Caledon village in 2002, when she was 40 years old, by which time she had packed in a lot of life. Known as Janey, she was popular and eccentric, a 'thalidomide baby' of the 1960s who had been born in Switzerland and overcame incredible odds to give birth to five children, all by Caesarean section. She spent much of her childhood in Caledon and went on to have a colourful life. She married her first husband, war cameraman Rory Peck, in 1981 and they had two sons, James and Alexander. The marriage ended six years later and he married his second wife, Juliet. He covered the first Gulf War in 1990 and worked in Bosnia, Afghanistan and the Soviet Union. In 1993, while he was on a job in Moscow, he was killed during a vicious gun battle outside the Ostankino television station. Janey's second husband was a landowner, Andrew Dobbs of Carrickfergus, but they divorced in 1999 and after a short sojourn in the US she had returned to Caledon to establish herself as an equine therapist and trainer.

Janey and her brother Nicholas had been brought up in the privilege of a bygone era and had both had a number of marriages, but they were very different characters. He inherited the title of the 7th Earl of Caledon in 1980, by which point he had married his first wife, Greek heiress Wendy Coumantaros. The relationship had ended by 1985 and four years later he married his second wife, the interior designer Henrietta Newman, a relationship that lasted until 2000. By 2008, when Janey went public about a row she was having with her brother, Nicholas was on to his third marriage, to Amanda Cayzer. The dispute between the siblings was over horses and the land that had been passed down to the eldest sons of the family since 1800, all five thousand acres of it. By the time the *Daily Mail* was ready to publish the article – headlined 'Earl clashes with his horse-mad sister' – Nicholas was in Switzerland skiing with Amanda and was incensed that he had had to take a call from a journalist. Janey had told the newspaper that her brother was refusing to allow her to ride her horses on the family's estate in case she claimed rights over it. 'This week, mother of five Lady Jane, known to friends as Janey, was sadly making new plans for exercising her 11 horses currently stabled in the yard next to the dower house where she lives . . . According to friends Janey has been forced to move her animals because Caledon has banned her from riding through his 250-acre deer park.' The article went on to compare Janey to Mrs Dashwood in Jane Austen's *Sense and Sensibility* and said that she had been rescued from her situation by a benefactor, Sammy Leslie of Castle Leslie estate, who had offered her stabling. From the Swiss Alps the Earl had been forced to explain:

I have done everything I can do to help my sister. There is no question of evicting her. She lives rent free and she can stay as long as she likes. But my hands are tied. If she rides her horses through the deer park, she eventually acquires rights to the land and the estate cannot allow it. It has to protect the land for the sake of future generations including my seventeen-year-old son, who'll inherit it from me.

The article and the public spat between the two privileged Alexanders became a talking point in the area, but the details did not go unnoticed by the young, ambitious jockey who'd come to live in the shadow of their vast estate. Johnny Creswell believed he had birthrights too and was determined he would claim them one day from his father, Herbie Lusby, at his ever-expanding Port Hall estate, which was fast becoming a recognised stud in Donegal. Creswell wasted no time introducing himself to Janey and charmed her enough that she had employed him to ride out her horses and even recommended him to her friend Sammy Leslie. 'He's a fabulous jockey,' she said. 'You just have to employ him.'

Creswell had very quickly got to know the affable and generous Janey and swept her off her feet with his charm. Janey might have been older than his own mother, but that didn't stop him flirting with her. Sammy Leslie was a different story – she wasn't so easy to flatter. Despite her upper-class upbringing, Sammy was notoriously down to earth and totally committed to the business of making her family estate a financial success. She'd grown up in Castle Leslie with her sister Camilla and mum Helen, the second wife of the eccentric Desmond. Her mother had been moved into the stately home after Desmond controversially evicted his first wife, Agnes Bernelle, and their children. While Sammy led what appeared a privileged life, the Leslie money was long gone and Desmond had worked hard to try to turn the estate into a business so it could be restored to its former glory. In an interview with the BBC years earlier, Sammy had described how she saw herself as a guardian rather than an owner of the home. 'Coming up to the end of the century the place is very much in the balance. In the next four to five years if we make it the place will be here in the twenty-first century and beyond and hopefully a lot longer.' A trained chef, she said: 'It's something I've always wanted to do. I've always felt very strongly about the survival of this place . . . I don't mind having all the people around the house as long as they respect it and they enjoy it. It's not like a home as such. I feel more like a guardian here to look after the place, rather than this is my home. I feel more like I belong more to this place than it belongs to me.'

In previous generations the Leslies and the Alexanders would have known one another and socialised together. But because of the Troubles Sammy and Janey had never met. After Janey returned to Caledon, Sammy decided to call on 'Lady Jane' and ask if she was up to help out in a community group in the village. She had nervously gone to the door and asked the unkempt woman who opened it if she could speak to Lady Jane. Her reply was 'Call me Janey.' The pair had rustled through the fridge and found some sausage rolls and a bottle of wine and become firm friends. Sammy did take Janey's advice to hire young Johnny to help her at Castle Leslie stables, but she was wary of his over-familiarity and kept their contact strictly business. She also recognised the charm that her friend had described but didn't think Creswell was the expert horseman that she believed him to be. 'He sat odd in the saddle,' she would later tell friends. 'But my God he could stay on.'

While an older woman like Lady Jane was useful to Creswell, it was the younger girls in the village who really looked up to him and made him feel powerful, girls like the Simpson sisters, Christina, Rebecca and Katie. Horse-mad since they were old enough to venture into Darton Ree, the sisters had grown up in a small bungalow right in the heart of Tynan, sandwiched between Dr Gillespie's house and the stables. Their home was one of four properties known as Taylor Cottages, built by Lord Taylor to encourage people to grow vegetables and fruit for the war effort. The houses were compact but the back gardens were huge. Throughout their childhood the girls spent all their free time with the horses, an almost inevitable passion as there was little else in the village for young people. Tynan had a once- or twice-daily bus service, but apart from that there was nowhere to go and little to do. The girls loved the outdoors and were rarely out of wellington boots, walking the fields and helping their father milk cows. They played with their cousins, splashing in paddling pools on summer days and dancing through puddles in the rain. At Darton Ree the eldest, Christina, first learned to showjump, displaying a talent and skill that would put the Simpson name on the circuit for years to come. Rebecca followed, and finally so did the youngest, Katie, who was a familiar face around the yard from the age of six. Like other youngsters drawn to Darton Ree, the Simpson girls helped out at the yard, where there was always a job to be done, and in exchange they would get a chance to ride a pony.

By the age of 14 Christina had dropped out of school and was working full time around the local yards, getting horses ready for events and mastering her riding skills. Katie seemed sure to follow in her sister's footsteps, even though she was only nine years old. She was tough and hardy and happy to muck out and mind the horses. Christina had formed a close relationship with Jill Robinson before Creswell came to work in the yard, but when he arrived the teenager developed a giant crush on the handsome jockey. From the minute he walked into Darton Ree Christina trailed around after him doing whatever she could to help him. She'd often travel with Creswell and Robinson to country events, leaving early in the morning and returning late at night. Sometimes she'd stay over at Caledon to save them the short journey to her home in Tynan. Creswell told Christina's mum, Noeleen, that he saw huge potential in Christina as a jockey and gave her tips and encouragement to perfect her riding and seat.

As he settled into Tynan he'd become ever more confident and outspoken and people either loathed or loved him; few people were neutral. Many found him arrogant rather than charming, but those who were taken in by him seemed to almost worship him. He liked the company of young girls and regularly made sexual remarks to them in the stables, commenting on their riding abilities and looks. Some welcomed the attention from the older jockey, but others thought he was creepy. Mothers too became the focus of his attention as he overwhelmed them with compliments about their talented daughters and their prospects of becoming champions. A very subtle form of grooming had begun.

CHAPTER 4

A WOLF IN SHEEP'S CLOTHING

While Creswell lavished attention on all women, he was undoubtedly a 'brunette man' and when he laid eyes on Abigail Lyle at a showjumping event in Belfast in October 2008 he wasted no time getting her number. Abi had long raven hair and big blue-grey eyes. She was from Bangor and on the same eventing circuit as him. Confident and bubbly, Abi had grown up with no connection to horses but she had embraced the hobby from a young age after taking riding lessons. Hers was a tight-knit family and she was particularly close to her older sisters, Rachel and Joanna, and had a great relationship with her mum Helen and dad David, who ran an advertising agency that would win awards for road safety campaigns on both sides of the border. While the Lyle family were known to be hugely successful, they had been overwhelmed by a terrible tragedy just years before, one that would mark each of them for the rest of their lives. For Abi, the trauma of losing her older brother to an overdose had seen her drop out of college and dramatically change career to the rough-and-tumble world of horse riding.

Despite an eight-year age difference Abi and her brother Matt had been particularly close growing up. He doted on his little sister and as a child nicknamed her 'Abi-giggle'. Together they would sit for hours watching *South Park* and drinking mugs of tea. Matt was a keen musician but as a teenager had started taking drugs, which quickly became a problem, and when he tried heroin he became hooked. The family supported him through rehabilitation, but he struggled to stay clean and when he was 28 he was discovered dead in his bedroom, having overdosed. A note about drugs and their impact on people and society lay on his locker. It was 29 August 2005, a date that would be forever branded on the souls of his parents and siblings.

Matt had fought hard against his addictions to drugs and alcohol and was in a period of recovery, but on the day of his death he'd bought a small amount of drugs from a local dealer. At his funeral, Abi, who was just 20, gave a eulogy about her big brother. Afterwards the family struggled hard to cope. Sister Rachel recalls:

He loved her. He doted on her so much. Abi was the youngest and she was really our pet so I don't know how she coped when he died. It was an awful time for everybody. You know it was so traumatic because he was found at home. I was in Dublin for the weekend but he was found in his bedroom. She got up at the funeral to read something and she just got up and said; 'I'm doing this for my big brother.' That was traumatic.

In the aftermath Helen and David bravely took the decision to speak out about Matthew and the struggles he had overcome to get clean and how he had been preyed on in recovery by local drug pushers, one of whom had sold him his last fatal hit. In a family statement the Lyles told of their devastation at the sudden death and described Matthew as 'much loved and treasured'. They said that he was a talented drummer and stated: 'We were all very proud of Matthew in his struggle to overcome drug and alcohol dependency. Our anger and bitterness is directed only at those who prey on young people like Matthew, callously seeking them out to push their poison for profit.'

A post-mortem showed that Matthew had been killed by tiny doses of morphine, dihydrocodeine and diazepam. Later, on a website dedicated to Matthew, the family posted the document found on his bedside when he died. He had written it when he was just 20 and when he was struggling with his addictions. In it he wrote with great maturity and understanding about the wider issues around drug use, including the funding of organised crime and terrorism. But he also recognised the effects of it closer to home: 'They can cause serious problems in relationships, split up families and sabotage physical and mental health. Britain has already suffered blows from the deaths of several teenagers after they had consumed ecstasy and left others brain-dead in wheelchairs or in mental health institutions.'

On the same website David recalled how on the last Saturday his son was alive he had talked to him about his hopes for a bright future, for getting fit again, for finding a job.

In the afternoon I drove him to get his bike fixed. We chatted about his hopes. When the bike was fixed he cycled home from the ring road and I drove back. When he got home he said; 'Dad when I was cycling through Bangor, one of the drug dealers stopped me and offered me stuff. They never leave me alone.' After midnight Helen and I were watching TV. He came in, wished us good night and said; 'I'm going upstairs to listen to my music.' He seemed fine, cheerful and relaxed. It was the last time we saw him alive.

Helen described how much she missed her beautiful child:

I miss everything about him – even the hassle and the rows and the tears . . . I am so glad I told him that I loved him the day before he died. He was standing in the kitchen making a cup of tea, I gave him a hug and a kiss and I told him that I was so proud of him because he had been clean for 3 weeks. But I couldn't help him, I couldn't fix him. I took him to detox and casualty on several occasions, picked him up from the police station, tended to his wounds . . . I miss him every day. He was so gentle. I imagine that like so many young people he thought he was invincible and that it wouldn't happen to him since he had escaped death before. He fought so hard to beat his addictions. And it was such a tiny amount of drugs that destroyed him in the end. That is what makes it all so tragic.

The bravery of the Lyle family and their openness about their terrible loss was regularly reported in the media. David conducted a number of interviews and talked about Matthew and other young drug users who are preyed upon by dealers, often in the grip of addiction themselves. As the owner of the award-winning advertising firm Lyle Bailie International, his was a powerful voice that proved that drugs know no social boundaries and can affect people from all walks of life and all backgrounds.

At the time of her brother's death Abi had been doing a degree at Queen's University, but she soon dropped out and began working at a Ted Baker store. She had always been keen on horses, having started riding lessons as a young child. She'd even convinced her parents to buy her her first horse as a teenager after delivering a presentation to them. In the aftermath of losing her brother it was the horses that seemed to offer her some comfort, as animals often do in times of grief. She spent more and more time riding and soon started to see her hobby as a potential career. She quit Ted Baker, landed a job in a yard in the North and began competing in showjumping events around the region. 'She kept coming back to the horses,' said Rachel. 'She'd always had a horse on the side and then she was working full time in a yard and it was around then that she met him.'

Johnny was funny and charming, loud and boisterous, and somehow made her feel that she was the only woman in the world. Abi was smitten and he managed to extract her number as they chatted between events. A flurry of texts followed and soon they were dating. Creswell was slim and good-looking and Abi told friends that he seemed very thoughtful and kind. He was well turned out, in an almost 'preppy' way, making him come across like one of the more privileged in the horsey set, and he was held in high esteem within showjumping circles. At 23, Abi was three years older than Johnny, but the age difference didn't bother her and his confidence made up for his youth. In fact, it was she that often wondered if she could possibly be good enough for him, something she had never experienced in previous dalliances. She'd had a number of relationships before they'd met but most had been students from her university days and none had seemed anywhere near as dynamic as Johnny. At home she told her family that she'd met someone special and Johnny was welcomed to the Lyle house, often joining the family for Sunday dinner. Around the table Creswell was engaging and polite and afterwards he and Abi would chat with the family in the cosy sitting room they called the 'snuggle'.

'He was very, very charming,' recalls Rachel.

He was very kind of hypnotic and he was a good-looking guy, before he put on the weight. He was well turned out but he had a really filthy car but all those horsey ones do. You know it was a big old jeep thing that was wrecked but when he stepped out of it he always looked very well turned out. We thought he was great and that he was lovely. He was always very smiley and when he was with you he really looked at you, engaged you. He was respectful with my father and there were no problems there, overall he just seemed like a really nice guy . . . I suppose he always seemed to be picking her up, taking her places, driving her to things so it was like he was always doing something for her.

As he neared retirement age, David began to wind down in work and booked a number of family holidays. Over Christmas Helen, David, Joanna and Abi travelled to Barbados; Rachel, a busy barrister, had to stay behind due to work commitments. On her return Helen admitted to the family that she wasn't feeling too good and hadn't been well for quite some time. She couldn't put her finger on what was wrong but decided to go to see her GP to discuss her symptoms. A series of tests followed but by New Year she was feeling no better. 'Mum was in that process of seeing the GP, coming back and then getting referred for a scan. But it was clear there was something seriously wrong,' said Rachel.

Abi had enjoyed the family break but was equally excited to get back to see Johnny. She wasn't a traditional romantic, but, as she had told friends, she fell head over heels in love with him at first sight. She couldn't explain it, she said, it was like she'd been transfixed from the minute she laid eyes on him. Such a close family would in other circumstances have noticed that Abi seemed to be staying away more with Johnny and spending less and less time at home, but the early months of 2009 were very worrying for the Lyles as Helen's health seemed to decline rapidly. By Mother's Day, 22 March, she was in a lot of pain, and when Rachel visited she was concerned both about a diagnosis for her mum and also the absence of her sister.

At this point we had all started to think what it could be that was wrong with Mum. I remember Joanna wasn't about on Mother's Day and Abigail wasn't about and Mum was annoyed and I had come down from Belfast and brought a dinner. We still had the grannies alive and they were coming for their dinner but there was no sign of anybody. With hindsight now, I know that it was after that first assault had happened. Abi had been staying with Johnny more and more and we did begin to realise at that point that something was up and we started to ask questions.

Despite the concerns around Helen's declining health, the family began to talk about Abi and her behaviour. Since returning from the Barbados holiday, she seemed to spend all her time with Creswell, but she didn't look happy. Joanna and Rachel tried to ask her if everything was okay, but the more they pushed the more Abi withdrew. 'That is when we became the "lying bitches",' said Rachel. 'So he went from being charming to calling us those names because we were enquiring if everything was okay. Abigail started to withdraw further and further and Jo and I started to kind of query it and ask why and we tried to figure out what was going on. But Mum was sick so there was a lot going on.'

That April, Helen was finally diagnosed with liver cancer and had to go to hospital for a week. While Rachel and Joanna were there all the time at her side, Abi slipped in and out while Creswell waited outside in his car.

It was fine, you know, she was in the hospital bed and we were waiting for the doctor to tell us what was happening and there was a general chat around the bedside. Abi was there but she was in and out while myself and Jo were there all the time. I can remember he would come and get her and she would have to go. The next thing that happened was the Paris trip, when Abi had to leave . . . And I remember that was really awful. It was really upsetting.

Despite Helen's diagnosis, David hoped that they could enjoy some time together, this time in Paris. It was there that the Lyle family realised that Creswell was not what he had first appeared and that Abi was in a toxic relationship. During the weekend away, which was over the Easter holidays, Abi was distant and preoccupied with her phone. Rachel and Joanna heard her rows with Johnny and heard him shouting down the phone at their little sister. They couldn't get her to spend time with them – she was always in her room – but on Easter Sunday, over lunch in a restaurant, things went from bad to worse. Abi announced that she had to cut the trip short and go home, claiming that she was busy with work. 'It was just hard and I'm not sure that she even wanted to come for lunch because she knew we would ask her about it. She knew we would poke her. She just said she had to go as she was busy but we knew the phone was going and we'd heard him shouting at her,' said Rachel. As they considered the events of the weekend, Rachel and Joanna realised that over the previous months, Johnny had stopped spending any time at their home, but with all that had been going on with Helen's health they hadn't noticed. They hadn't picked up on Abi's withdrawal into herself and her strange behaviour either. Under their noses he'd isolated their little sister and was being anything but charming with her. 'It was the ideal time for him to get her where he wanted her to be. Things were fraught. I think then it went very bad very quickly. There were no real visible physical signs up to that point, but by June we could see it.'

At the start of June the family gathered in a restaurant to celebrate Rachel's birthday, an event which would mark the last time they all had a meal together. It was a lovely occasion, but at the table Abi began to open up to her family about what had been going on with Johnny; that he could be abusive and violent and that on one occasion he had smashed her head off the dashboard of his car. The family were shocked but relieved that Abi had finally confided in them that her relationship with Johnny wasn't all that it seemed. Rachel said:

The good thing about Abigail is that she can't hold her water. I just remember us being in the restaurant and we were glad that she had told us. We thought that would be a fresh start and that opening up about what had been going on would help her move away from him. We felt a sense of relief and we thought it was going to be over. But when the meal finished she went off again.

But that night she went back to him. Helen's health was going downhill very quickly and she was undergoing chemotherapy every two weeks. Rachel was trying to take Fridays off to be with her mum and after the first couple of sessions of chemo there was good news; the tumour had gone down. But the reprieve was short-lived. Helen soon became even more sick. 'I remember being up at the cancer centre and they were saying you know you could have a bit longer but within a few weeks she was clearly very bad again.' The final trip Helen would take with David, at the end of June, was to Antibes in France, where he was doing some business. She was in pain and spent most of her time with Joanna, who had accompanied her parents on the trip. When the couple returned home to Bangor, Helen found Abi in a terrible state. Johnny had beaten her black and blue. Helen phoned Rachel to tell her that Abi needed help and a solicitor so she could get a protection order. Unknown to the family, Helen had only four days to live.

By the following day Abi had found a solicitor, but since there was no court sitting she had to wait another 24 hours to get a non-molestation order against Creswell. That afternoon, 1 July, Helen was rushed into the Marie Curie Hospice in Belfast for pain management. Over the following 48 hours her health went rapidly downhill. Joanna and Rachel were at her bedside, along with husband David, but Abi was distracted and was in and out of the room. Finally the family were called to say their goodbyes. Helen's death was shockingly sudden, the cancer a swift wave that raced through her system and took her life in a flash. At the hospice Rachel and Joanna rang Abi's phone over and again and eventually she showed up at 4am, a baseball cap pulled firmly down over her face. For the second time the Lyle family would have to dig deep and reach out to one another for support. And it was at that very moment that Abi seemed to become darker and even more withdrawn. Rachel remembered:

I think we thought they had separated but we realised that they were back together on the night of Mum's death because we couldn't get hold of her. It was four or five in the morning when she came to the hospital and it was then we realised that they weren't separated. He didn't show up at the hospital but at that stage he'd given her the choice, you know that it was us or him. And then it just got worse, so much worse until August. The truth is that in the weeks after our mum's death he really went for her.

CHAPTER 5

A CALL FOR HELP

Just weeks after her mum's untimely and shocking death, Abi was punching Nuala Lappin's phone number into the public payphone in Caledon. Shoeless and terrified, she listened to the ringtone and was relieved when Nuala picked up. 'Please help me,' she wept down the line. 'He's beating me again.'

The rows had been intensifying, of that there was no doubt, but there was something about this one that had brought Abi to her senses and to the payphone on the main street of the small village, one of the few quaint throwbacks to the past that actually had a use. Abi was shaking, but she was angry too. The fact that he had taken her boots, her keys and her mobile phone and locked her out of the house, humiliating her for all to see, had somehow brought her to her senses. She was going back to the house to get her things, but that was it, she was done with Johnny Creswell.

Less than 20 minutes later Nuala arrived at Chestnut Manor and rapped at the door. A police officer since 2002, she was the first specialist domestic violence officer in Tyrone. Creswell pulled open the door and glared. Nuala could see Abi cowering behind him down the hallway as he blocked her way.

'What do you want?' he growled as Nuala reached into her back pocket and took out her warrant card.

'Abi, get your things. You're coming with me,' Nuala said.

Creswell took another step towards her. 'She's going nowhere.'

'Abi, you are coming with me. Get into the car,' Nuala directed, taking control of the situation.

Creswell puffed out his chest and again stepped towards the officer, red-faced and fuming. Nuala took out her gun and shouted 'Armed police!' Abi, holding her mobile phone, slipped around Creswell and went to the car. As the pair drove away the phone started ringing. Then came the texts: 'I love you Abi. Come home.'

Abi was lucky that the PSNI domestic violence liaison officer appointed to her case after she was granted the non-molestation order in the Belfast court was one of the best. Nuala Lappin was highly trained and skilled in the complexities of domestic abuse and coercive control and well versed in the patience and support often required for a victim to seek formal help. She also had a bubbly, vibrant personality and a positive outlook on life that was infectious. Nuala knew about Abi's personal circumstances and she was confident that, even though the Lyles were going through a terrible time, they were a close, supportive family and would be there for Abi when she needed them. Nuala hadn't been surprised that Abi returned to Creswell, despite the non-molestation order; she knew that he had a particularly tight hold on her. But she had been on high alert for a call. She worried for many of those in her care but found Abi's case particularly troubling because of the volatile relationship and her fears about the capabilities of Creswell. When the call came Nuala wasn't too far away, but she had no idea where Caledon was, never having been there before and had to navigate her way to the best of her ability, hoping to find Abi safe and alive.

As they drove towards Dungannon police station, Nuala considered the Johnny Creswell she had met at the door. He was prepared to square up to her, an armed officer with a warrant card. He was also still sweating and flushed from the display of temper that had played out behind the walls of the little terraced home that day. Abi sobbed at her side while Nuala urged her not to answer the calls but to save the texts coming in from him on her phone so they could be used as evidence.

Creswell's black tempers had always been sparked by very little, but they had become worse in the previous weeks as Abi was torn between grieving with her family and her relationship. The rows had intensified as Creswell had issued her with ultimatum after ultimatum – it was her dad and sisters or him. The final row had gone on for hours, but Abi was determined that it would be their last. She would never let Johnny Creswell take advantage of her again. As they drove to the police station Nuala comforted Abi, reassuring her that everything would be okay, and as she did a dawn of realisation seemed to descend on her. What had happened to her in the previous nine months? How had she ended up in such a toxic relationship? Why had she continuously gone back to Johnny, despite the violence and cruelties he'd doled out to her? How had she actually survived some of those attacks? And the biggest question of all – Why had someone like her become a victim of domestic violence?

Nuala knew a lot from all her training and vast experience as a liaison officer. First up, Abi would need a lot of help and counselling to see her through the coming months, particularly if they were going to get Creswell to court and into prison, something she believed was vital for the safety of other women around him. She also knew that domestic abuse cases are complex and that victims question themselves as much as they do their abuser. From the minute she had met with Abi and heard about the beatings she had suffered at the hands of Creswell she knew that hers was a high-risk case. As a police officer, her first responsibility was to safeguard Abi. Then she would help guide her through any statement she made. There was an urgency, too, to gather that statement and to arrest Creswell. Time was not on Nuala's side.

At Dungannon police station, Abi took a seat in an interview room and began telling a dark story of a seemingly ordinary relationship which had turned dark without warning. Abi had never before been in a violent relationship, she told the police, and had only ever had verbal disagreements with partners in the past. She'd had no warning whatsoever about the first assault, which had taken place on St Valentine's Day, six months before, and just three months into her relationship with Creswell. He had turned on her while driving his car and beaten her senseless. They'd had a row earlier in the day, but he'd bombarded her with texts and then offered to collect her, but then he'd become jealous and accusing and demanded to see her phone. He'd started to speed, frightening her, as they drove towards Caledon on country roads and turned one corner so aggressively that her phone had flown out of her hand, landing on the back seat of the car. He'd started to punch her in the stomach while he drove the car, he'd pulled her hair and then bashed her head against the passenger window. All the while he was shouting and yelling and calling her names. As Abi tried to catch her breath he again grabbed her long hair and this time brought her head down face first onto the dashboard. Abi had curled up, trying to protect her body, she told the officers, as he hit and punched her over and over again. Afterwards, she said, she was in complete shock and scarcely knew what had just happened to her, but as quickly as it had begun Creswell had cooled down and started to apologise to her profusely, reassuring her that he'd only 'lost it' because he loved her so much and because she was so special to him. He told her he couldn't live without her and wouldn't ever lose his temper in such a way again. Abi had forgiven him and she had believed him when he said it wouldn't happen again.

But time and again he'd done the same thing. After that St Valentine's night, the beatings had become regular and they had quickly become part of the fabric of their relationship. There was a clear pattern; he'd fly into a jealous rage over something he'd accuse Abi of or something he read on her phone, which he regularly demanded she hand over to him. He would lash out and punch and stamp on her, using her long hair to drag her about and pulling her to the floor. His demeanour during his rages was often one of high excitement and he regularly appeared sexually aroused. Afterwards he'd apologise and make Abi feel special again by telling her that she was his 'number one'. As she pieced together the previous six months of her life she could see the pattern herself and how the violence had quickly become something that happened more and more regularly. She could see how she'd stayed away from home sometimes so her family wouldn't see the bruises and so they wouldn't ask her if she was okay. He'd turned against them, too; he said her parents were needy and accused her sisters of interfering in their relationship.

Over nine hours and between breaks Abi's story spilled out, and as she came to the end of a gruelling 19-page statement, she was exhausted and needed to go somewhere safe while the PSNI took the next steps.

In the pages of Abi's statement, what stood out for Nuala was that clear pattern of behaviour that she had articulately explained. A lot of the triggers that flipped his switch appeared to have something to do with Abi's mobile phone, which he regularly took from her and checked. On one occasion, Abi had told officers, she was enjoying a day off work and was having a nap on the sofa in his house as she'd been out with school friends the night before. The night had been fun and she had bumped into a boy she hadn't seen in years. They had chatted and exchanged numbers and he'd texted to say he was happy to see her. The text on her phone was anything but flirtatious. It simply read: 'Really lovely to run into you last night. I hope all is well.' As she slept Creswell had picked up her phone and keyed in the code to unlock it, something he regularly did without her permission. On seeing the text he had become enraged and as she dozed he'd begun to storm around the house. She'd awoken to find him closing all the blinds and locking the doors. He'd found her car keys and hidden them. Purple with rage, he'd screamed at her that she'd be getting a 'hiding', that he'd seen the text on her phone. Abi had begged him to calm down and tried to explain that the boy was simply an old school friend, that their relationship was nothing but platonic, but he wouldn't or couldn't listen. For hours he beat and whipped her as he gave in to an insatiable rage that terrified Abi.

The car, too, featured regularly in the incidents Abi had described in the course of her interview. He often drove at speed while beating her, almost like he was riding a horse and whipping it. On one occasion he'd driven Abi over the border to beat her and he'd regularly denied her her possessions during his rages, taking her keys, her phone and even her clothing. After every incident Creswell would apologise and promise to never hurt Abi again and without fail he'd use the charm and charisma that had bowled her over in the first place to make her forgive him. As Abi described the levels of violence during her interviews a stark realisation had dawned on her. 'He could have killed me any of those times,' she remarked to Nuala. 'Any one of those beatings could have been my last.'

As the law stood at that point there was no way Nuala could use the pattern of abuse to make an overarching case against Creswell; it would be more than a decade before Northern Ireland recognised domestic abuse and coercive control as criminal offences. Instead, Nuala knew she would have to take apart the statement and identify individual criminal offences, which she would then have to forward to the Public Prosecution Service, which would then decide whether any charges could be laid. In order to prove and back up Abi's claims, her phone and the reams of messages between herself and Creswell would be vital. Comments she had made to her family could also be used, along with GPS location trackers that would show when the couple were on the move. The pair had been prolific communicators, and even during Abi's time in the police station Creswell had sent a number of texts to her phone telling her to come back, that he was sorry.

The most serious offence that stood out from the statement, from the point of view of bringing charges, was the incident when

Abi had been taken by car to a forest at Castle Leslie estate, where she had undergone the most severe of all the attacks. Castle Leslie was over the border into the Republic and therefore in a different jurisdiction. Creswell had been working on a casual basis at the estate in County Monaghan and sometimes rode out the horses there for Sammy Leslie, having been recommended as a fine horseman by her pal Lady Jane Alexander. It was a place he was familiar with, but it was also totally secure and patrolled by groundsmen. There had been a row, sparked by jealousy and accusations, and he ended up collecting Abi at her home in Bangor. The assault started in the car. Creswell had stopped off at his home in Caledon, ordered Abi to stay in the car and then driven on to Glaslough, to a wooded area he'd told her was Castle Leslie, where he'd assaulted her over a three-hour period. At one point during the assault, her statement claimed, he'd removed her shirt and used it to tie her to a tree as he whipped and beat her. Then he'd tried to hang her, hoisting her up in the air as she grabbed to protect her neck. Abi was terrorised during the attack, she had stated, and had begged repeatedly for her life. Because he had taken Abi across the border and held her against her will it was possible to get a kidnap charge against him, a serious offence with a sentence ranging from 12 months to life imprisonment. Nuala could also identify in the statement numerous other incidents of criminal assault and threats to kill.

The following day, 17 August, with Abi in a safe place under the protection of her family, Creswell was arrested and brought to Dungannon police station for questioning. He was feeling confident and assured. He had a solicitor present but despite his advice, Creswell believed he could handle the situation himself.

'Abi is a nutter,' he said. 'You've no idea what this girl has put me through mentally . . . She self harms . . . She's away in the head . . . She has had serious bereavements . . . There are drugs in the family.' His blue eyes gazed at Nuala as he put on the charm offensive for the officer. Again and again his solicitor advised him not to answer questions, but Creswell knew better. Over a six-hour period, Creswell leaned back in his chair, his legs splayed. 'The wee girl is cracked up on me,' he said. 'I can't get rid of her. I know it's not a good relationship but I've sat up with her night after night.' Quizzed about how Abi had got her bruises, he answered that she regularly lay on the floor and rolled about to cause herself injury. At one point he stared directly at Nuala and said: 'Look at me. I can have any woman I want. Women love me. Let's get this sorted and I can get back home. I've barely slept.' Asked about Castle Leslie, he suggested that Abi had made it up and that she had gone there herself and rolled around in the forest to pretend he had beaten her. But when asked about how he had helped Abi, given his narrative of her mental health breakdown, Creswell couldn't show he had tried to get her to a GP or spoken to her family. Neither could he explain why he hadn't taken her to hospital or had any of her injuries checked out.

His arrest did nothing to quell the support Creswell enjoyed from those closest to him. While he was in custody Jill Robinson phoned the station saying she believed Abi was a chaotic character and she wanted to make a statement. She was advised that she could only give a statement to Creswell's solicitor, if she so wished, because the PSNI was 'victim-centred'.

It quickly became apparent that Creswell was not going to be released and would have to go into custody while he waited to get a bail hearing. Abi's father, David, reached out to try to protect his youngest daughter. He phoned James Creswell, Johnny's grandfather, who had reared him like his own son. It was an awkward phone call but David tried to keep things as pleasant as he could and suggested that between them they make sure that Abi and Johnny kept away from one another while the dust settled and the legal process continued. Creswell was curt and said he was surprised by the story that Abi had given to police. He told Lyle that his grandson had completely denied the allegations and indicated that while he would try to ensure that the pair were kept apart he would be defending him in court.

CHAPTER 6

GOSSIP AND
A COURT CASE

It wasn't long before the story about Johnny and Abi was being whispered in equestrian circles throughout Northern Ireland. Abi and the Lyle family remained tight-lipped about events at Chestnut Manor for fear of undermining the legal process. But the Creswell camp were clearly spinning hard and soon Abi was being portrayed as a jealous and possessive girl who couldn't cope with her boyfriend's popularity with other women. A new relationship he was in with the teenager Christina Simpson was being cited as the reason for the blow-up at Chestnut Manor. Abi and he, friends of his claimed, had had a volatile relationship throughout their time together and had regularly been at loggerheads in a passionate and toxic way, but getting the police involved was an indication of Abi's jealousy that he had moved on with Christina and left her behind.

Word around the Darton Ree yard was that Johnny was being framed and he would defend himself all the way, and he had plenty of support behind him. And he had convinced many people. Even Dr Gillespie said he'd give him a character reference should he ever go before the courts. Perhaps it was hard to believe that the charming Johnny could be violent to his former partner, surrounded as he always was by a bevy of women who seemed almost starstruck in his company, and supported by some of the stalwarts of the equine industry. It was easier, in many ways, to believe the stories about Abi and her jealousy.

Creswell was remanded in custody and later that week appeared at East Tyrone Magistrates' Court in Dungannon seeking bail. Present in court were his friend Jill Robinson and his new partner Christina Simpson. Over the course of the hearing some of the details of what had gone on behind the door of Chestnut Manor began to emerge. During the hearing the court was told that Creswell was facing a string of charges relating to alleged violence against his former partner. There was a total, the court was told, of 13 charges, 11 of which centred on crimes against 24-year-old Abi. Creswell remained in handcuffs while the court heard that six charges related to assault causing actual bodily harm between dates in February and August of that year. One of those, the court heard, involved a claim that he threatened to throw Abi in a bath of acid. Two of the charges related to a threat to kill her and a further two to kidnap.

Nuala Lappin took the stand. She said Creswell had punched and kicked his victim and forcefully restrained her in his car at his Caledon home. The police had been told he had regularly struck her while he was driving and at one point she had tried to escape from the car. The officer said that the assaults would generally last an hour and the victim hadn't reported them as she was living in fear of Creswell. She said Abi had been threatened in March and again in August when the final alleged incident had occurred. Over their time together, she had told police he'd told her not to tell anyone of the assaults and said he'd murder her if she did. Even from jail, the court heard, he'd warned her he could get at her.

As the bail hearing proceeded the court was told that Creswell was 'extremely jealous and possessive' and had continually checked Abi's phone. On 7 June he'd lost his temper, the victim had said, and thrown her phone against the wall and then stood on it to make sure it was broken. Objecting to bail, Nuala Lappin said Creswell presented a high risk of interference with witnesses and the injured party, and she told the court he had tried to contact her by text several times while she was giving her statement. His defence solicitor revealed that at the time of the last assault Abi had been granted a non-molestation order but that when it was served on him she was at his home and still in contact with him.

James Creswell, Jonathan's grandfather, took the stand and said he wanted the district judge to hear what he had to say. He said he'd had a call from David Lyle to inform him of the charges against his grandson. The pair had met in Caledon, he told the court, and agreed that they would try to get Jonathan and Abi to stop the relationship for six months while decisions were made by the court. James Creswell told the court that he was 'shocked and stunned' by the allegations and that he was totally bewildered. Appealing to Judge John Meehan, he said, 'Everyone loves Jonathan. He has represented Ireland and Europe in horse riding and brings out the best in awkward people and horses. He is not bad-tempered.'

Judge Meehan considered his position, saying:

This is a very distressing situation, whatever was going on between the parties. It is my job to look at the evidence put forward and it is clear there is no doubt there is cause to connect the defendant. The injured party made a detailed statement, which alleges a controlling relationship. She is able to describe the defendant's alleged method in threatening to kill, referring to acid or bleach in the bath and his potential to place her in it. Equally he says she harmed herself. There is the suggestion of a psychologically bizarre range of control of power expressed when he wouldn't allow her access to her car.

In the body of the courtroom journalist Tanya Fowles was frantically taking notes. A native of Tynan, she knew of Johnny Creswell and some of the rumours about him mistreating horses and making crude remarks to young girls. She knew Dr Gillespie too, and some of the others who had given references as to the good character of the man in the dock. Tanya worked for the local newspaper, the *Impartial Reporter*, but was also a stringer for the national newspaper media and the BBC. She was a multi-award-winning court reporter and knew the law inside out. She also knew about domestic violence and had personal experience of being in an abusive relationship herself, something that had steered her career into being something that was very victim-led. Tanya knew Nuala too, from bumping into her around the court circuit, and sometimes they'd have a coffee and a natter. That morning Nuala had stridden into the courtroom, spotted Tanya in her seat in the press bench and walked straight over to her, telling her to watch out for her bail case and the evidence that was likely to come out around it. 'You will be interested in this one if you attend,' she had told her.

The District Court was a hive of activity as usual and Tanya was always one to sniff out the best story. She'd usually review the court lists and recognise some of the more familiar names, but that morning she decided to take Nuala's advice and throw an eye on the Creswell bail matter. As the case came to a close and Creswell was refused bail, Tanya went back over her notes. The evidence so far was simply shocking, far more serious than many other cases she had covered. The threat of the acid or bleach bath and the terrifying journey into the forest at Castle Leslie were above and beyond what she would regard as a 'normal' case of domestic abuse. Tanya put a note in her calendar to make sure she was in attendance the next and every time the case was called.

Days later, at the High Court in Belfast, Creswell was granted bail on a surety of £750 and on the understanding that he would stay at Chestnut Manor in Caledon and report to the PSNI once a week at a specific date and time. He was ordered not to attempt any contact with Abigail Lyle.

In the days after his release from jail following his dramatic arrest and period in custody on assault charges, Creswell went straight back to work in the stables with tales from his stint in prison and some of the criminal characters he had met there. The confidence he exuded in relation to the upcoming case he would have to answer certainly did nothing to quell the rumours around Abi Lyle's state of mind and it was generally accepted that his defence would tear apart any allegations that she had made. As if to hammer home the narrative that his new relationship had caused a jealous blow-up he was ever more attentive to 15-year-old

Christina Simpson and the pair spent more and more time together riding out and working around the stables. Besides, Creswell didn't have time to be maudlin or to worry unnecessarily about something that was likely, in his mind, to blow over. After all, he was back in the saddle, back on the track and he was determined he would soon make his name as a champion race jockey.

Since riding his first point-to-point at Tyrella in 2007, Creswell had been working on his reputation as a jockey and he was determined to bring home a winner. Months after he was released from jail he succeeded on both fronts when he had a surprise win on the Ian Duncan-trained Inverlochy Lad, which he rode to victory by a half length at Kirkistown in north Down. Jill Robinson and Christina Simpson were both there as he strode around the winners' enclosure. Creswell hoped that would begin a winning streak, but by December he was being placed again, ninth at Navan and seventh at Downpatrick. Over Christmas he celebrated in Tynan and attended the hunt and on 27 December at Down Royal he was pipped to the post for second place on Inverlochy Lad again. And whenever he got the chance he would tell anyone who would listen that Abi Lyle was an obsessed lunatic out to ruin his life and his career.

By February he was before Omagh Court in County Tyrone where he pleaded not guilty to the catalogue of abuse towards Abi over a six-month period. He was intent on going to trial, and his supporters were out in force to defend him. He was remanded on bail and appeared again in May when the case was mentioned. All the while he continued to race at point-to-point events. Between February and late August, when his case was called for mention, he competed in five races at Downpatrick,

Down Royal and Wexford in the south-east of Ireland. On 8 August he saddled up on Finnegan Express, trained by Patrick J. McKenna, but came in a disappointing eleventh. The race would be his last for almost a year and a half, because in September Creswell did something unexpected – he changed his plea to guilty. That meant that a number of the more serious offences, including the kidnap charge, were dropped. He'd taken it to the wire and only pleaded guilty the day after a jury had been sworn in to hear the case, but nonetheless he'd benefit from his admission. Guilty pleas are always welcomed by courts and seen as a mitigating factor for a defendant facing a jail term on the basis that they have saved the state the cost of the trial and a victim the indignity and trauma of giving evidence and reliving their ordeal. Pleading guilty, by its very nature, would usually mean an admission of fault or blame, but while Creswell admitted his guilt to the court, in private he spread a very different story, telling his employers and his friends that he had been backed into a corner by Abi Lyle and that she was prepared to lie about him in the witness box. While that meant he had to admit to some of the charges, he claimed, he'd get the whole thing over with quickly and be able to get back to work.

For Abi, the plea was a mixed bag. She had been dreading a court case and facing Creswell while reliving her horrendous ordeal. Despite relocating to England and undergoing a huge amount of counselling, Abi was apprehensive about giving evidence. She understood the court system, largely due to the advice and wisdom of her barrister sister Rachel. She knew that a guilty plea meant that Creswell would get a lesser sentence and little media attention. In true Lyle style, just as her parents had in the aftermath of the tragic death of her brother Matthew, Abi decided she was going to take control of the situation, forgo her anonymity and go public with her story to make sure that she could make maximum impact with it.

As Creswell's sentence hearing opened at Dungannon Crown Court before Judge David McFarland, a small crowd gathered, including Abi's family and liaison officer Nuala Lappin. Journalist Tanya Fowles was there too, the date firmly fixed in her working calendar. The court heard that the Crown was willing to keep four charges on the books, including two threats to kill, while Creswell was willing to plead in relation to five of assault. Simon Reid, for the prosecution, told the court that in respect of the remaining counts it was the statement from Abi Lyle, made in the aftermath of her rescue from Chestnut Manor the previous August, that formed the basis of the case.

He set out the facts, telling the judge that the relationship between Abi and Jonathan Creswell had begun in October 2008 but on St Valentine's Day 2009 he was violent to her for the first time. On that day, he said, they had broken up but later met in Bangor in the early hours of the morning. Creswell picked Abi up and they drove off, but all of a sudden he started to strike and punch her around the head and body. He persisted with the assault during the course of the car journey, despite her begging him to stop, the barrister told the court. At Moira, located on the opposite side of Belfast to Bangor and about 45 minutes into the journey, Creswell had suddenly changed and apologised to Abi. The court heard that she was in pain and had bruises on her face as a result of the attack. The next incident involved Creswell arriving at the Lyle home in Bangor to pick her up. Initially, he seemed friendly but in the car made it clear he was going to attack her. In her statement, Abi had described how she had started crying and asked to get out but he had driven on towards Caledon, all the while being verbally abusive to her. Near the house he had punched her in the body and the head and on arrival at Chestnut Manor ordered her to remain where she was in the car. He went inside the house, the court was told, and when he returned she was sure that he was about to attack her again. In her statement Abi had described how she had begun to scream and tried to escape from the car but that he had pulled her back by the hair. Then he drove off again, this time to the woods of Castle Leslie, where he had proceeded to assault her again.

From her seat in the press bench Tanya Fowles glanced at Creswell over her glasses. He was young-looking, red-faced and with floppy blond hair, which gave him an innocent look. He was tiny – a jockey – and on the face of it seemed incapable of such violence. In the dock he remained motionless, but in all her years reporting from court Tanya could not recall a case as concerning. While he was no longer facing charges of kidnap or threat to kill, the details of the attack at Castle Leslie were shocking. She would later recall:

It was the strangulation and the viciousness and violence of the attack that I really couldn't believe what I was hearing. When I heard the evidence that was set out the first thing that struck me was taking her over the border; that was a pointed and manipulative thing to do to take a victim out of a jurisdiction. He had also trapped her in the car a number of times and wouldn't let her out. I was trying to think how he'd got there and where the forest was. Was it on the estate or somewhere else? Had he pre-planned where he was going or was this on the spur of the moment? The assault had gone on for hours and Abi had told the police that he was sweating, he was that exerted. It was terrifying for those of us listening to it so I could only imagine how Abi must have felt. He wasn't a big guy, he was only a wee jockey, but what he had done, and what he admitted to doing, was sinister in the extreme. And yet there were women there supporting him. I remember seeing Jill Robinson and Christina Simpson in the courtroom. They were there for him.

The court heard that the next incident was again at his home. Creswell had become enraged during a conversation when Abi had related to him details of a previous relationship she'd had. He'd punched her in the body and the head and she had been so frightened that she'd ran from him around the house. The fourth incident before the court was also at the house, when he'd confronted her about names on her phone and went on to slap and drag her around. The next charge, the court heard, related to a petty dispute over a TV which escalated to the point of him hitting and dragging her. That time, the court heard, bruising on her head and body had been observed by family and friends, which corroborated her account. She had eventually got a non-molestation order, but had returned to meeting him. One day in his house he had demanded to see her phone and attacked her again. He threatened her that he had filled a bath of bleach and would put her in it. Prosecutors for the Crown conceded that they did not think he had actually prepared the bath but that he had punched her in the stomach. She had attended an accident and emergency department, where bruising to her head, nose, chest and back was confirmed.

Again Tanya looked over at the young man in the dock. 'A bath of bleach? That was insane. I mean even to think about that let alone to threaten someone with it. It was definitely the worst case I think I'd ever heard,' she said later. As a seasoned court reporter Tanya knew that Creswell's guilty plea meant that he was not going to be facing a hefty sentence for the attacks. She understood sentencing guidelines better than most and knew that often a judge's hands were tied if mitigating factors weighed heavily for the accused. In the case of Creswell, she considered, his guilty plea, his age, the level of support and character references for him, and the fact that he was a working jockey with his life ahead of him were all going to go in his favour.

But there was more to come. The details of the last attack still had to be heard and the court was told that despite the emotional pain and fear, Abi had returned to Creswell once again. The last attack lasted days and only ended when he went out and Abi managed to escape to the phone box from where she had called Nuala. 'The victim, despite pleas from her family, who had become aware late on of the true nature of her relationship, to stop seeing him, had continued nonetheless to continue, thinking he would stop. This is a pattern familiar in domestic violence. She did ultimately realise the true nature of the relationship and made her complaint,' Reid told the court, adding that had the matter gone to trial there would have been other powerful evidence, including witnesses who had seen her injuries and a 'half-confession' to her father.

Defence lawyer Patrick Taggart said that Creswell had no record of violence and was a skilled and talented jockey. Abi Lyle had made a full physical recovery from her injuries and Taggart argued that when contact was made in the aftermath of the non-molestation order his client would argue that he was told it was no longer standing. A psychological report commissioned for the trial found that Creswell was of low average cognitive ability and someone who displayed weak literacy skills, particularly in regard to spelling; however, he was not found to have dyslexia. Taggart said: 'His background is that he is someone who, at a very early stage, decided school life was not for him and the equestrian world took over. He has represented Ireland at an international level and has been involved in showjumping from the age of nine. He intends in the future to develop into a trainer himself, having previously just ridden for others.' The psychological report went on to deal with issues around alcohol or substance abuse, neither of which was found to be a problem for Creswell, and it stated that while he accepted he had a propensity for aggression he couldn't give a reason for it.

'If we look at his record there is no violence,' Taggart pointed out to the court.

This was a toxic and tragic relationship for both himself and the injured party and there has been nothing since that. It was an intensely emotional relationship and very little of his reactions can be deemed rational. That in no way takes away the effect that his actions had on the injured party and he is conscious that this happened at a very difficult time for the Lyle family. Throughout the report, he accepts responsibility but cannot explain it – it seems to be [the] case he can't explain it. He is unable to go into any great detail except to say that he seems to be caught up in this relationship. I know the report was at pains to point out that it is a grave matter that he went on to offend on foot of a non-molestation order [but] there was an element – evidence – she was partly involved in contact there as well which led to further offending.

He described himself . . . when asked about his involvement in offences, and I quote: 'He cannot be sorry enough.' He is unbelievably sorry. He claims he thought he knew himself better and he became emotionally distressed at the interview when challenged. I think it is a case, your honour, when he simply can't define what exactly caused him to act the way he did but at no stage is he trying to defend what he did . . . The author of the report . . . states that whatever the circumstances of this relationship it is clear that Creswell's behaviour was violent and reckless and abusive and without justification. He is not assessed as someone who is a risk of serious harm to the public . . . His behaviour is an aberration that is confined to this relationship and this relationship alone. I ask your honour to give him credit for his plea.

References describing Creswell as a hard worker and an aspiring jockey were handed to the court from world showjumping champion Dermott Lennon, businessman John Chambers, employer Dr Fitz Gillespie and Dublin Horse Show Chief Steward Gerard McCloskey, as well as a family friend called Mr Rose. Taggart told the judge that custody was an option but that his client should be given credit for his plea before the trial date. As Judge

McFarland sat to deliver his judgment Tanya Fowles glanced over to Creswell once more. He stood in the dock with his head down as he awaited his fate. Dressed in a baby blue jumper and tie, he looked innocent, almost cherubic. Abi's ordeal had really resonated with her because Tanya had once been the victim of domestic violence herself and had found herself in a coercive relationship back when she was 21.

I did have a violent relationship myself many years previous . . . and it was strange and similar because you do lie for them and cover for them. It was the amount of lies I told, including to my parents, which had surprised me. And you know there were a lot of injuries . . . I could remember one particular occasion, and this is why I really resonated with Abi, because he had turned on me while he was driving one day. He was raging about something and he was left-handed but he let go of the steering wheel and punched me with his other hand. He'd got me right across the nose and the blood flowed and he panicked. And to my dying day I will remember a lemon-coloured Mini coming the other direction towards us and me thinking 'someone please stop', yet knowing in my head that even if they did I would say it was an accident. But there was a lot of blood, so my clothes were covered when I went home that day. It was bad and my mum said 'Holy God'. But I lied and lied and lied and said I'd fallen forward in the car and that it was awful and everything. For me the problem came when it stepped outside me. My parents were on holiday and I'd gone around to feed the cats and pick up the post from the door and he had to come in and I was rearranging the post from about three days' worth in order of size and he asked what I was doing and I told him. But he thought I was looking for secret letters. He insisted on opening every letter in case I had some admirer. All of them were either bills or something to do with my dad's business. And I was standing watching him and then he reared up and my parents had a TV in the corner of the room and Daddy had made a panel to set the video underneath because he didn't want a table. So he kicked off and wrecked the living room. And I can remember him kicking under the video and it flipped up and something changed because, weak as I was, he'd gone too far.

Like I had gone through a stage where I couldn't eat and I had been in permanent fear in my stomach but I just turned on him physically and managed to put him out of the house. It was my parents' house he had wrecked and it had taken that. I locked him out of the house and I sat at the door and I was still there five hours later. He kicked it and thumped it and did everything. Outside he said he knew where the spare key was and then he started to say he forgave me and could I let him in. He was saying: 'Tanya, I can't manage without you.' But I never answered him. He was trying to put his hand through the letterbox and everything but I just sat there with my back to the door and I said to myself: 'It stops now.' So for five hours I sat there and it was the summer and I had a short denim skirt on. And it was only when I looked down I could see there was a big trainer mark on my leg where he had stood on me and I hadn't even noticed him doing it. It was this big mark and I was just sitting there looking at it.

I sat and sat and sat, and it became completely clear. It was like a fog lifting but it took him to do something to affect my people and not me. And outside he gurned and wailed and threatened suicide. That was it and I wasn't afraid of him anymore. I don't know where I had got the strength to put him out but I did. Eventually I went to Mum and Dad's room and listened but as night went on I could feel all the muscles get sore and stiff. The phone rang non-stop but my brother was due to come home. Knew when he came home I could answer the phone again. And, you know, something like that, it leaves you that you can spot it and you know when someone else is lying and covering up and excusing. I will never forgive myself for being so stupid and vulnerable, but there you go. I could understand Abi.

Justice McFarland began his summation and Tanya continued to take notes: 'Your victim is Abigail Lyle,' the Judge began, looking directly at Creswell.

You and her commenced a relationship in and about October 2008 when she was twenty-three years of age and you were approaching your twenty-first birthday. You both had a professional interest in horses and you had substantial experience as a showjumper and as an eventer. Your main focus is as a jump jockey at point-to-point and National Hunt and I understand that you wish to continue and further your training. I accept this is a hard profession, both in relation to the preparation for events and the participation in them. As I understand it, you are a young man with no alcohol problems or drug issues and you don't smoke. You are clean-living from that point of view. However, you have had difficulties in relation to this relationship you were having with Ms Abigail Lyle and, in your own words, and I accept this, at times you 'just lost it' which is a statement you made to your probation officer. During some arguments you indulged in unacceptable behaviour and this was sustained over a period of time. The assaults occurred over six months and resulted in injuries to Ms Lyle, one of which required hospital treatments.

The first incident is a fairly typical example of your possessive attitude and your violent conduct towards Ms Lyle. It was the early hours of the day after St Valentine's Day. You had a row on St Valentine's Day and you told her to leave, which she did, and she had returned home to Bangor. Your house was at that stage in Caledon in County Armagh. You had begun to pester her with text messages and ultimately in the early hours of the next morning, that is the fifteenth of February, she had agreed to return to you. You drove from Armagh and she got into the car but on the return journey you started to assault [her]. The assaults were punches and at one stage you stopped and punched her again. At another stage she tried to escape but you pulled at her hair. There were also moments of intimacy during that journey and this was fairly typical of what happens over the next six months. The assaults were sadly repeated and to some extent the violence escalated because it did involve kicks as well as punches and hair-pulling. Fortunately for her, and indeed for you, the injuries that she sustained were fairly minor physical ones. At one stage she obtained a non-molestation order, which is an order from the court forbidding you to assault her, however that did still not protect her, although I do accept that she did expose herself unnecessarily by returning to you.

Sadly, Ms Lyle's conduct is typical of ladies trapped in this type of relationship where there is sometimes a willingness to return to an abusive relationship and ignoring advice from family and friends. It is perhaps a naive faith to think things will return to normal but ultimately she returned and exposed herself to further harm, but this in no way explains or condones your conduct. The aggravating circumstances in this case are that the violence was perpetrated in a domestic setting. That is the first aggravating circumstance and the second aggravating circumstance is that this was repeated offending, there are six counts and they span a period of six months. And the final aggravating circumstance is the fact that the last two assaults were in breach of a non-molestation order.

The judge then laid out the mitigating circumstances. First, Creswell's guilty plea, which, he said, meant that Abigail Lyle did not need to attend court and give evidence. 'It was a rather belated plea, but it was a plea nonetheless and acceptance by you that you had committed these offences,' he said, pointing out that one defence statement Creswell had lodged stated that the injuries were self-inflicted. 'I'm sure it was a difficult time for Ms Lyle coming up to this hearing, but your plea of guilty, albeit late, avoided the need for her to attend, give evidence and be cross examined so you will be given some leniency for that plea of guilty.' Second, the judge said, his almost clear record would be taken into account; and third, his age. In the dock, Creswell was 22 years old, but he had been just 21 at the time of the incidents, had good work records and was well thought of by some people within the horse riding and training community, the judge remarked. Before sentencing Creswell, Judge McFarland said:

Under the terms of the Criminal Justice Northern Ireland Order my first task is to assess whether or not you are dangerous, that is after your conviction for the bodily harm offences. The statutory test for this is whether or not there is a significant risk of serious harm. I have considered all this and my view is that while there is potentially a risk of future harm, I don't think I could categorise that as a significant risk or serious risk so in the circumstances I find that you are not dangerous as defined by the 2008 Order.

As for the sentence itself, had this been a single offence or indeed two offences it would have been possible in my view, taking into account all the mitigating circumstances, for me to impose a non-custodial sentence. However, there were six assaults in this case which occurred over six months and this is in my view a case that demands an immediate custodial sentence. The length of that sentence is being determined by all the mitigating and aggravating circumstances. There is in my view a need to assert to you and to others that this type of violence perpetrated against females in a domestic setting will not be condoned by the courts and those who perpetrate it should expect to receive, and will receive, an immediate custodial sentence. However, I am bearing in mind your age and that a lengthy sentence would make it difficult for you to be rehabilitated back into the community. So in all the circumstances the sentence I am going to impose under the 1996 Criminal Justice Order is six months in custody. So in practical terms it is a six-month sentence, but you may be subject to remission, but that is a matter for the prison service and the Minister for Justice. Take him down.

Tanya Fowles felt six months was a very short sentence, given what she had heard in the courtroom, but she also understood exactly why it had been decided on. The public were unlikely to hear the exact details of what had happened at Castle Leslie – the attempted strangulation, the hanging from a tree – but all of that had been covered under a simple assault charge and the judge had been left with no option but to follow the guidelines laid out for him. 'He was a good judge, the best in the circumstances. It was just the way the sentencing had to go. Everything was in Creswell's favour. It's hard for the public to understand that but that is how it goes. A custodial sentence at all was a win in that case,' she explained.

One of the things that changed a lot in the aftermath was the introduction of new laws that came in the years after that, one of which was non-fatal strangulation. Because Abi was choked, we had heard that she was choked until she passed out. Had that been a stand-alone charge as opposed to what it was then, which was assault occasioning actual bodily harm, that would have changed things significantly. Plus he'd been charged with kidnapping Abi but in his plea deal, in admitting the assaults, he got the kidnap charge dropped which related to the driving over the border and detaining her in the car in the process and smashing her phone. These are echoes that would come back.

The young man in the dock had given her a creepy feeling since she first laid eyes on him and just one month before the sentence hearing she'd seen him competing in a county show. 'He was on quite strict conditions that he wasn't allowed to do certain things but I'd seen him showjumping and he was in great form and surrounded by girls and that was just a month previous. He wasn't a man that seemed in any way perturbed by even the thought of prison,' she said. One way or another Tanya was sure of one thing – her gut told her he'd be back before the courts again – but at that point she had no idea the impact he would have on her life or others'. 'I don't think anyone was under any illusion but that Abi came very very close to dying. He seemed to enjoy putting people in fear. That was a frightening aspect. As for Nuala, who removed Abi from the house, it's quite extraordinary that he took the position he did with her and squared up to her. I'll be honest, I've known her for thirty years and wouldn't dare square up to her. This man only came up to her chest but he fully defied her. He was like "you get out of my face". That bravado and defiance would only develop more because no lines were drawn.'

Outside the court Abi held back the tears as she appealed for other victims to come forward, saying:

This kind of thing happens all too often . . . but it shouldn't happen to anyone . . . ever. Today shows that the systems in place to help people work, so there is no reason to take this kind of abuse of any kind. Without the support of Nuala from the police domestic violence unit, Women's Aid and my close family and friends I would never have gotten through this.

Later that day, her sister Rachel would recall how Abi phoned her mobile, something reserved for emergencies. While the pair were in constant contact most days, it was always through texts and lengthy voice messages. A call meant something was wrong. Rachel was busy, but as soon as she got free she called her sister back. 'Rachel,' Abi said. 'Mum is dead. She's gone.' Rachel took a breath before soothing her crying sister. 'Yes, Abi. She has been dead for a year.'

CHAPTER 7

BACK IN THE SADDLE

Two o'clock in the afternoon was playtime for Johnny Creswell. At two o'clock on the button he'd drop whatever he was doing and head into the barn near Gillespie's Yard where great laughter and merriment could be heard as women gathered to see him perform. Sometimes a horse would be the butt of his often cruel jokes, but more often it would be a woman. He liked to pull ponytails and make crude remarks about body shapes and double entendres about riding and getting into the saddle. His delivery was quick and usually with a smile, leaving many unsure what he had actually said. Around him women would laugh, particularly those closest to him. Since he'd returned to Tynan and his home at nearby Caledon after a three-month stint in Maghaberry prison he'd become more popular than ever. In fact, he wore his conviction like a badge of honour and his short time behind bars with pride. Although he'd been handed down a six-month sentence by Judge David McFarland at Dungannon Crown Court, good behaviour and remission had meant he'd served just 12 weeks and had been out in time for Christmas 2010. He'd actually been welcomed home with a party at the Armagh City Hotel organised by his horsey friends. Among those in attendance was the ever-present Jill Robinson and a new brunette, Hayley Robb. Robb, from Banbridge, was 17 but would quickly drop out of school and a promising academic career to spend all her spare time in Johnny's company. Christina Simpson was there too, vying for a position as his steady girlfriend, despite being six years younger than him.

Johnny always had plenty of stories to tell but fresh out of prison he was brimming with talk to keep those around him agog. There were anecdotes about Michael Stone, the loyalist militant who had killed three people at an IRA funeral in 1988. He'd been released under the terms of the Good Friday Agreement but had been jailed again, charged with attempted murder of Sinn Féin leaders Martin McGuinness and Gerry Adams at Stormont buildings in 2006. In prison Stone had taken to painting and while they simply shared the roof of Maghaberry Prison, Creswell's stories would make those listening think that they were cellmates.

Then there was Colin Howell, the dentist from Coleraine whose murderous affair with housewife Hazel Buchanan had been one of the most sensational stories Northern Ireland had ever seen. Howell had entered Maghaberry as Johnny neared the end of his short sentence and he'd quickly become the talk of the prison as fellow inmates strained to look at the unlikely killer in their midst. His religious background and the double murder he committed so that he could continue an illicit affair in the heart of Northern Ireland's Bible Belt assured him celebrity status. Howell and Buchanan had started their relationship back in 1990 after meeting at their Baptist church and when their respective partners, Lesley Howell and Trevor Buchanan, were found in a fume-filled car a year later, their double suicide was blamed on an apparent pact made as a result of a clandestine affair. The story was all but forgotten for the next two decades, but in January 2009 Howell handed himself in to the police, admitting that he'd gassed his former wife and his then lover's husband and had fooled police into believing they had taken their own lives. Howell and Hazel Buchanan (later Stewart), who'd embarked on a doomed relationship in the aftermath, had both been brought before the courts in February 2009, while Creswell was still denying his own assault charges. In November 2010 Howell pleaded guilty to double murder and was soon sentenced to a minimum of 21 years behind bars. Creswell was quick to realise that stories about his crimes were sure to hold a crowd. Like a soldier returning from war, Johnny's homecoming to Tynan was celebrated and that Boxing Day he led the hunt, proving that being a jailbird had done nothing to his ability to stay on a horse at all costs. If anything, his time in the clink seemed to give him an even greater swagger than before.

As far as Johnny and his network were concerned, Abi Lyle and her tall tales were long gone, a distant memory in the tight-knit circles where they worked and socialised. Despite her efforts to highlight her ordeal at the hands of her one-time boyfriend, Abi's reputation was in tatters. With no support and shunned by many in Northern Ireland's equestrian circles, she had been forced to relocate to England. But she hadn't gone away altogether. In September 2011, a video popped up on a website called thedetail.tv featuring an interview with her. In it Abi bravely revisited a terrifying time in her life and tried to make sense of how she had come to accept the serious levels of violence regularly doled out by Creswell during their nine-month relationship. The details were far more graphic than anything reported at the time of the court case. She described how she was beaten for hours at a time, regularly strangled until she went limp and how she thought she was going to die during the incident at Castle Leslie forest. 'He beat me up for two or three hours. It was a cold night and it had been frosty but he was wearing a vest by the end of it because he was sweating so much,' she said. In the interview, with journalist Kathryn Torney, she said: 'I couldn't even explain why I fell in love with him so quickly. He just did things to make me think I must be very lucky to have him and I always thought I mustn't be good enough for him.' Of the Valentine's night attack she said: 'I just remember thinking; "Oh my God, what's just happened?"' Abi revealed her terror of being strangled, which began to happen each time there was an attack: 'To me that was worse than taking a punch,' she told the journalist. In great detail Abi tried to make sense of why she stayed in the relationship.

> The only explanation I have for putting up with this sort of violence as I did, is because I was put down so much, that I felt like a million dollars when he was nice to me. The feeling I got when he said he was sorry and that he loved me was amazing. It was the biggest relief in the world and that's what I really fed off and I became dependent on it in a really bizarre way.

Abi's experience at the hands of Creswell has been echoed countless times. Years later, a Department of Justice document, *Experience of Domestic Violence: Findings from the 2011/12 to 2015/16 Northern Ireland Crime Surveys*, revealed that a little more than 12 per cent of the population aged 16–64 had experienced some form of domestic violence from a partner, namely non-physical abuse, threats of force, with women over twice as likely as men to be victims. Just like Abi, an over-whelming majority, almost 75 per cent, said that the worst single incident of violence and abuse had happened in a relationship with the perpetrator being a male partner. Police had been made aware of only a third of those cases. However, it was clear from a table of 'risk factors' associated with domestic violence and abuse identified in the document that, apart from being in a relationship at the time, everything else about Abi Lyle, as a victim, and Johnny Creswell, as a perpetrator, was out of sync with the norm. Factors identified showed that single parents were at higher risk and rated higher, along with married people and those from lower-earning households where the annual income was below £15,000.

In many ways Abi Lyle was ahead of her time in speaking out as she did to support domestic violence awareness. It would be another six years before women began to find their voice when it came to calling out dangerous and seemingly untouchable men like Johnny Creswell. Abuse allegations made against film producer Harvey Weinstein in 2017 turned the Me Too movement and its hashtag viral. American actress Alyssa Milano started the trend by suggesting on Twitter that if all women who'd been sexually harassed or assaulted used the #MeToo status, it might show the world the magnitude of the problem. Celebrities like Jennifer Lawrence and Gwyneth Paltrow soon weighed in and the backlash led to the end of some of the biggest careers in Hollywood.

But when Abi sat in front of the cameras to tell her truth it was way before doing so was part of any movement empowering women to speak about wrongs done to them. As her sister Rachel recalls:

Abi had done a lot with Women's Aid and there were lots of articles and stuff about her. But she was so brave speaking out back then and it was because of all the help she got from her PSNI liaison officer Nuala Lappin and from Women's Aid and all the counselling she had got, particularly in England. When you think about it she had to go to England to get away from Johnny and the attitude against her. But speaking out wasn't done back then. It's only really in the 'Me Too' era that you have people being more comfortable about it. Nowadays we have coercive control legislation but we didn't back then.

Abi came across as confident, resilient and sincere. A number of national media followed up on the story, but Camp Creswell held firm. While her story may have made some impact and some head-lines it had no bearing whatsoever on those who lived just to be close to Johnny Creswell. In fact, since his stint in jail, his celebrity status seemed to have increased and despite what should have been a black mark on his character he appeared to have become even more irresistible to the women who surrounded him in growing numbers. Not long after his return to his rented house in Caledon his teenage girlfriend Christina Simpson all but moved in with him. Despite just turning 16, Christina was finished with schooling, concentrating on a career as a rider and totally embedded with the older Creswell and his best pal Jill Robinson and their day-to-day lives working in stableyards and attending events. Christina followed Creswell around like a love-struck puppy, hanging on his every word and happy to do anything to be near him. But she wasn't alone and often had to compete for his attention with the older Hayley Robb, whom he had met on the equestrian circuit. From the high-class Weavers Meadow in Banbridge, Robb was academically gifted. She had obtained nine GCSEs and was studying for her A levels with a view to becoming a physiotherapist when her world collided with Creswell and her plans and ambitions were quickly put on ice. Just as with Abi Lyle, the attraction was transfixing, inexplicable and would ultimately prove to be toxic.

In many ways the long hours and hard work of stableyards suited Johnny, particularly when it came to managing his growing stable of women. The work gave him some cover; since Christina, Hayley and Jill were all working in the same place he could keep tabs on what they were doing and who they were talking to. He somehow managed the women so that each seemed to accept the others in the hierarchy of his world. Jill Robinson was aloof and the most confident around him. While he might criticise her in company or make cruel remarks about her looks or clothing, he showed the least sexual interest in the oldest of his female companions and she was free to pursue other relationships. Christina was delighted to be in his presence and vied for his attention like the giddy teenager she was, but it was clear that he had total control in their relationship and he ordered her about like a staff member. She'd groom his horses, clean his boots and wait patiently for a moment of kindness to make it all worthwhile. But Christina was no shrinking violet either and ever since she was a young girl she had seemed to know how to get what she wanted. Hayley Robb didn't look unlike Abi, with a mane of dark hair and a wide, pretty face. She could have had her pick of boyfriends but instead she seemed satisfied to take the crumbs from Johnny's table and he loved to boast about how they would meet up for sex in a stableyard or on the bonnet of his car. Together the girls travelled with Johnny as he began to compete again.

From the outside theirs looked like an idyllic lifestyle. They were surrounded by horses and kids attending pony clubs, who looked up to them as older and more experienced riders. While they were all still working at Darton Ree, Johnny also rented a corner of the yard for himself where he hoped to turn his dreams of becoming an owner and trainer into reality, and in order to inveigle himself more deeply into privileged society he became a prominent member of the South Tyrone Hunt. From early on, Johnny recognised that to gain access to young women and to their parents' money he needed to charm their mothers and, to a lesser degree, their fathers. Saturday was 'cinema club' when Johnny and his women treated the younger kids to a day out with popcorn and fizzy drinks. At 2pm those who were going with them would be ferried to the movies. Later, back at the Caledon house, before they were collected by their parents, he'd entertain them with loud jokes and barrack-room banter. There were whispers of inappropriate behaviour with young girls, many of whom were brought up to his bedroom and shown pictures of him in jockey silks and on horseback. One guest would later recall how as a nine-year-old she was told she was his 'special girl' for the day. Some parents didn't like the vibe and attempted to challenge Johnny, but since it was not clear what was actually going on they were often made to feel that they were the ones with the bad minds. After all, Johnny was surrounded by adoring women; how could there be any suggestion that he was inappropriate with younger girls?

Others watched Johnny from a distance, finding him creepy and sinister. One local man, known as a horse whisperer because of his incredible skill in calming animals, didn't like what he saw. This man, a quiet and gentle character, had little power in the equestrian community and certainly wasn't someone who would be listened to, but he did privately try to warn parents not to let their girls near Johnny. He'd watched his behaviour with women and with the younger girls who loved to ride horses. He'd been very concerned when he stumbled on the jockey putting young children on thoroughbred stallions, notorious for being aggressive and unpredictable. While the children were thrilled with their chance to sit on the huge horses, the man knew that it was dangerous to let inexperienced young riders on their backs. Sometimes the man warned the younger kids not to go near Johnny's corner of the yard and he did what he could to steer them away. He told whoever would listen that he thought Johnny was cruel to the horses, turning to ketamine to tranquilise them for simple procedures around their teeth and hooves rather than calming them so they could be treated without drugs. He'd seen him whipping the animals as he guided them over ditches and dykes. Later, as he spread his wings and moved to other yards and stables, he would be known for using steel poles on jumps while training horses, a method which would hurt the animals should they knock them.

In the small pond that was the villages of Tynan and neighbouring Caledon, Johnny was the ultimate big fish and he held himself with confidence in company. But his ability to forge friendships was limited and while he could pass muster when dealing with his own sex, in particular owners or trainers and other jockeys, he never had any interest in hanging out with men. A non-drinker, he looked down on those who finished their day with a pint and he didn't like his women drinking. One strange friendship that Johnny developed was with a young English lad, known as an oddity, who spent summers with his grandmother in Tynan. Aaron McWilliams was shunned by teenagers his own age and came across as a social misfit, but he adored Johnny, laughed at his jokes and trailed around after him when he wasn't babysitting children to earn some money from summer work.

While he might not have been a man's man, Johnny's success with women and his ability to charm them was a skill that crossed generations. Not only were women his own age bowled over by his attention, older women were drawn to him too. Mothers of young girls attending pony clubs were told that their daughters were naturals and rising stars sure to become champions. Compliments were whispered about their youthful appearance, often glances were exchanged and stares lingered that second or two too long. Even Lady Jane Alexander was beguiled by Johnny's charms and tried to give him additional work with her horses. While she was approachable and down to earth, her friendship with Johnny raised eyebrows, such was the vast difference in their social backgrounds. Johnny was loud and proud of his closeness with Lady Jane and when she let him borrow her car he regularly drove up and down the village of Caledon at speed, doughnutting it, to make sure everyone could see.

For much of 2011, after his release from prison, Johnny had stayed local to Tynan and neighbouring Caledon and kept his head down as the dust settled on his brush with the law. It was not long before there was far more scandalous and headline-grabbing news than his rocky relationship to occupy the chattering classes. For the equestrian set, *Game of Thrones*, which was putting Northern Ireland and its horse industry on the map, was top of the small talk agenda. Featuring scenes shot from the streets of Belfast to the World Heritage Site at the Giant's Causeway on the Antrim coast, the landscape of Northern Ireland had been transformed into the hottest new film set on the planet and as the cult around the US medieval fantasy series took off so too did the area's reputation as a hub for film and television. Stories around why and how HBO had chosen Northern Ireland to shoot the award-winning show, based on the novels of George R.R. Martin, were better than any tourism marketing that could have been dreamed up. With it came employment: the show created plenty of that, and particularly when scenes involving horses and riders were being shot.

The details of forbidden love and murder tumbling out from the courtrooms where Colin Howell and his former lover were tried and into the newspapers were also keeping everyone interested. Following Howell's plea of guilty to the murder of his wife and the husband of his former mistress, Hazel Stewart had been brought before the courts for planning the killings, but she denied the charges, claiming that she was vulnerable and weak in the face of her 'obsessed, calculating and controlling' lover. A lengthy trial followed her not guilty plea and the sordid details of the couple's murderous extra-marital affair spilled out. Apart from the titillation around the affair, the fact that the duo had managed to trick police into believing their spouses had committed suicide and had got away with it for two decades fascinated the public. The case placed the focus on the police and how they had been tricked into believing the story spun by the killers. In March 2011 Stewart had been found guilty too, and at the age of 48 she was sentenced to life in prison after a 15-day trial that would inspire at least one TV series.

Criticism came fast and furious. Outside the court Detective Superintendent Raymond Murray, who had led the investigation, told the media he understood the anger of the victims' families about the original investigation, which had concluded the pair died by suicide. However, he added, 'I think we've got to remember 1991 was a very different place in Northern Ireland – there were 102 terrorist murders alone and CID were a lot more stretched than they are at the minute.' But a lack of resources wasn't going to cut it when it came to the big questions around how the police had been tricked into believing a story fed to them by two cold-blooded killers. What followed was a damning report by the Police Ombudsman detailing just why Howell and Stewart had got away with murder for so long and what lessons needed to be learned from the police's failure.

As the memory of his stint in jail faded, Johnny was determined to get back in the saddle and end his break from the racetrack. By 2012 he was riding for David Christie, one of the most prestigious trainers north of the border. But in March, riding Slieve Kirk at Down Royal, his horse was pulled up. Later that summer he was forced to pull up again in Listowel in County Kerry on Bonapartes Retreat. He had slightly better luck on trainer Liam Lennon's Maple Valley Gale, placing fourth in Wexford later that year, and days later riding Howwolduno in Galway. His last race of the year saw him placed sixth at Down Royal. Despite his brush with the law he was regularly risking getting pulled by the Gardaí and the PSNI, driving chaotically and often without tax or insurance. In September 2012 he was forced before the courts in Donegal for driving without proper insurance. Judge Sean MacBride said that Creswell could pay a €300 fine in the form of a donation to Donegal's GAA Centre of Excellence in lieu of a conviction. At the time he was caught Creswell, then 23, had been driving from Monaghan to the Galway Races and gave his address as Chestnut Manor in Caledon. During the short hearing Judge MacBride asked Creswell how the horse he was riding had fared in Galway and was told it had not won. Dismissing the prosecution, he said he'd give the young trainee jockey 'a chance' and wished him 'every success in the future'.

It was a bad start to the new year in 2013 when he fell at Naas on Lennon's A Special Lady. He came fifth in another race and pulled up in a third. But while he wasn't dazzling with his performances on the track, his good looks did turn him into a would-be champion when he was picked by an advertising company commissioned to make an advert for Channel 4 to promote the Grand National, held at Aintree in April. The advert to promote the festival saw Johnny, clad in yellow and green silks, carried shoulder-high after a seemingly historic win. That same year, Lady Jane Alexander married Johnny's first employer, Dr Fitzroy Gillespie, in a small ceremony in Tynan Church. It was clear that Johnny had lost interest in their small-town lives. He'd started to spread his wings for more reasons than one and by 2014 he was riding for Victor Robinson's Armagh stables and for Liam Lennon from Newry, County Down. His form was poor and his best race saw him coming in sixth, while he twice trailed home in seventeenth place, but he was growing out of Tynan and into new stableyards where nobody knew his form.

While Johnny was struggling to make a name for himself as a point-to-point jockey his women were proving to be the real stars of both the track and the jumping circuit. Jill Robinson and Christina were building reputations as very talented jockeys, and among the big-name trainers they were riding for was Andy Oliver. Oliver had trained as an equine vet and travelled the world before returning to Ireland and his home farm in Caledon. By 2010 he had begun to enjoy big race wins and was growing his stable. In a later interview with the *Irish Independent* he would describe his business as like 'managing a Premier League football club'. He gave an insight into the early mornings and hard work that were necessary to make it in the business.

It's very much a seven-day week. They start early. They are fed at five-thirty every morning and then they're put into automatic walkers to warm up. The main body of staff come in at seven-thirty a.m. and start riding out. We would ride six lots a day and they all have to be cleaned out, mucked out, fresh water, fresh hay. The horses are then cooled down, fed again at lunchtime, checked over, groomed in the afternoon with a lot of them getting out to paddocks and then fed again at nine o'clock. It's a very structured regime and it's just about keeping the horses interested, keeping them healthy and obviously getting them fit. That's just your day-to-day routine. On afternoons where you'd be racing, the ones that are running would be sent off.

It was on an Oliver horse, Above The Law, that Christina recorded her first winner in 2014.

While his girls were winning prizes and landing plenty of work, Johnny saw himself as their boss and manager and his own role as training them to reach their potential; and his aim was to buy and train his own horses. He promoted himself as someone who could break a horse for an owner or rich family, which earned him money on the side. While breaking a horse was historically a harsh battle of wills between human and animal using methods of force, it was far more acceptable in modern times to use skill and patience to build trust. The use of physical force to teach obedience had also made way for communication and mutual respect. But while the industry had progressed, and even the language around taming a horse had changed to 'starting', Johnny didn't have time or the personality for any of it, preferring to succumb an animal by beating it, ultimately demanding respect in the same brutish way he did from his women. Many owners who sent their horses to Johnny, or entrusted him with the process of getting them ready for riding or hunting, found they returned with a different spirit.

He may not have been a champion jockey, but on horseback Johnny was confident, and his fearlessness was not up for debate, particularly when riding to hounds, an activity in which he shone. But while there was prestige and local celebrity in hunting, there was no money in it. Johnny needed cash to realise his vision and ambition of reaching the very top of the racing world. He wanted his own stud farm, just like Andy Oliver, and to be a man who would be revered and respected among women and horses. If he reached the top, he knew, they could all stay together, Jill, Hayley and Christina – and the newest addition to his entourage, Christina's little sister Katie.

CHAPTER 8

A RITE OF PASSAGE

From the beginning of his relationship with teenager Christina Simpson, Johnny had charmed his way into her family. At the time her parents' marriage was coming to an end, so tensions were high and emotions frayed. The union of Noeleen and Jason Simpson had always been a turbulent one and the girls, Christina, Rebecca and Katie, were well used to getting out of the house when rows kicked off. They'd grown up in the heart of Tynan village in a small bungalow, the location of which had made it inevitable that they would be drawn to the stables and to the riders. The Taylor Cottages were sandwiched between Darton Ree yard and the Gillespie family home where Dr Fitz had lived with his wife, Barbara, until her death in 2007. The cottages formed a central part of the small village, sitting directly opposite the church and graveyard. As a small child, Christina toddled into Darton Ree stables to gaze at the horses and the riders who sat on them and as she grew she would help out, doing odd jobs, and sometimes ride the horses out into the fields. Rebecca soon followed her and as a very young child Katie too would spend any spare moment she had with the ponies, picking up tips and skills from the older riders who hung out at the stables.

Noeleen eventually bought her girls a horse between them, which they fought over, all showering it with love. The girls grew up close to their grandparents Colm and Angela, who helped out, along with aunts and uncles who lived nearby. When Noeleen, a qualified chef, fell pregnant with her last child, a boy she would call John, she split up with Jason and moved to the nearby village of Middletown and opened a takeaway there. Like many dedicated riders, as a teenager Christina's interest in horses outweighed her interest in school and she started to explore ways of earning a living by competing as a way of displaying her riding and showjumping skills. Noeleen would later tell a BBC *Spotlight* programme, 'My girls knew how to stick up for themselves. Especially Katie, even with boys, when she was younger playing. Rebecca or Christina might have run in but Katie would have held her ground. When she was younger if her dad was working nights milking she'd have been standing in the hall with her wellington boots on waiting for him so she could give him a hand. She was very good. A very good child.'

For Katie the small world of Tynan was her whole life. She shared a love of horses with her best friend Chloe Scott and together the pair started to ride and compete in small pony shows. Classmates and soulmates, they treasured the rosettes they won at local events and talked non-stop about their favourite ponies and the unique personalities each had. Sometimes, if there was a row at home, Katie would sleep over at the Scotts', where there was always a freshly made bed for her. The Scott home would become her sanctuary, a place where she felt safe, loved and wanted. Chloe later said that her friend was only around ten years of age when she noticed that Johnny Creswell had begun to control her.

While her older sister Christina had become an accomplished rider through grit and determination, Katie was an absolute natural from a very young age. She was fearless and she loved the horses, stroking and soothing them, her gentle nature inspiring their love in return. As Johnny cemented his relationship with Christina, he soon began to take a huge interest in her little sister Katie, who was strong and hardworking, despite her age. He'd often summon her to help him and often she would stay late in the yard with him mucking out, even on school days. 'Nothing stood out about him in the beginning,' Noeleen told *Spotlight*. 'Nothing at all. Just how nice he appeared, how charming and Jill [Robinson] too. She was older and all smiling and you'd think if Jill was a nice girl he couldn't be that bad because he was with her.' Not all the family liked Creswell, however, and he did have a tendency to divide opinions wherever he went. Katie's aunt Colleen McConville said, in the same documentary, 'He was very arrogant and I can remember rolling my eyes at him because I couldn't stand the way he was in people's faces.' Those who weren't charmed by Johnny felt he was sleazy and uncouth, always quick with a crude remark. But he didn't care about fitting in – Tynan had become too small for him and his ambitions lay elsewhere. He was never going to be a champion jockey, and he was constantly struggling with the weight restrictions, so he wanted his own land where he could make the transition to a serious player in the equestrian industry. By 2014 he had managed to buy a number of his own horses and stabled them in David Christie's yard in Fermanagh. That same year Christina, aged 20, had recorded her first winner and was being pipped for national success. An interview with Andy Oliver, during which he complimented the young rider, made it into the

Irish Independent. 'She has been with me for three or four years. She is a great girl and a great worker, fair play to her she gave him a great ride,' he said. That win was only Christina's eleventh career ride.

Johnny regularly accompanied Christina to race meetings, when he wasn't working by himself, and had begun to train both her and Katie to jump. Jill Robinson was permanently in his company, as was Hayley Robb. Although he was still only in his 20s, his confidence had continued to grow and he'd become more boisterous and crude in his interactions with other jockeys, while exuding charm when he spoke to pony mums and the female riders he paid special attention to. His absolute conviction in his own worth created a barrier to those who might have considered challenging him, and often it was the giggling women who surrounded him, who hung on his every word and tolerated his crude language and behaviour, who stopped anyone stepping in to defend their honour. Johnny seemed to have an opinion on everything when it came to 'his' women; their hair, their makeup, their choice of clothing. He was obsessive about their mobile phones, often publicly demanding they hand over their phones so he could check who they had been texting and what social media they had been watching. They never seemed to stick up for one another, often appearing grateful if he was picking on someone else. He had his favourites, different ones when the mood took him. But it was behind closed doors and in lonely stables where Johnny had created a very dark world where coercive control was a tool he was perfecting. What had happened to Abi Lyle during her relationship with Johnny Creswell was now the world of many others.

In wider society in Northern Ireland domestic abuse and crimes against women and, more important, the PSNI's response had become a talking point again. In November 2015 the PSNI Chief Constable George Hamilton warned that due to workload pressures the force had difficulty resourcing vital case reviews that could help prevent domestic violence killings. Hamilton said that he would have to prioritise legacy issues over probes into the background of domestic abuse-linked murders and manslaughters. At the time an average of five people were killed every year in Northern Ireland by a current or former partner. Calls had been made for the establishment of domestic homicide reviews following the case of Arthur McElhill. The convicted sex offender had torched his house in Omagh in 2007, killing himself, his partner and their five young children. An independent investigation into the tragedy had found that health and social services had failed to reach some of the most basic standards of care, and it made over sixty recommendations to agencies supporting women and children. Eight years on, the Department of Justice said it was set to introduce new legislation to make it a legal requirement for a domestic homicide review (DHR) to be carried out after every domestic violence death to identify lessons to be learned and help prevent future tragedies. But the PSNI Chief Constable warned that while he was supportive of the introduction of DHRs, the police service had resource issues. While she had survived, the violence doled out to Abi Lyle could have killed her, she believed, but like many issues around domestic violence that detail had fallen between the cracks. Creswell's ex-girlfriend was all but forgotten, but instead of being shunned by his community he had returned to Tynan like something akin to a celebrity and instead of keeping quiet about the dark secret in his past he had even begun to boast about what he had done. He had started to use Abi Lyle's story and the details of it as a way of threatening others.

By 2015 Creswell was working in a stableyard in County Antrim while Christina was building her point-to-point career at race tracks across Northern Ireland and into the South. Young Katie too, not yet 16, was often in the yard with him and under his guidance. Late that year a couple from Scotland, who would later agree to be known as Sarah and Ian, came to work there, both securing employment and accommodation. It didn't take long for Sarah to notice Creswell as he was always the centre of attention and was loud and brash. In the mornings he led the group of young jockeys who rode out to give the horses their first exercise of the day. 'Everyone seemed to treat Creswell like a supreme being. They couldn't get enough of him. He was arrogant and egotistical. He and Christina came as a team and she was always there too. We avoided him. Neither of us were part of the circle and that suited us fine,' Sarah would later tell Tanya Fowles. Soon Johnny began to make crude remarks and sexually inappropriate comments to Sarah, who ignored him until one day he separated her from the others and started to talk about his previous convictions, about how he'd been accused of 'battering' his ex-partner. He said he'd 'supposedly' threatened to put her in a bath of bleach, which he denied, saying he could just have easily 'drowned the bitch' in water. 'He was proud of what he did and enjoyed talking about it,' she would later say. 'He was laughing and used derogatory language about the girl. I remember he said "the only mistake I made was not finishing the bitch off."' Stunned into silence, Sarah couldn't believe what she was hearing, but she was even more shocked by the reaction of those within earshot. She tried to walk away, but Creswell blocked her path, laughed and made hand movements as he described in minute detail how he had strung his partner from a tree in the forest near Castle Leslie and how he had used her own shirt to tie her up. Unknown to Sarah, who had never heard of Abi Lyle or the case, all the details were absolutely accurate.

Shocked and speechless, Sarah again tried to walk away, but this time he stood in front of her and exposed himself. 'He was ready for sexual activity. He'd done his boasting and bragging, which I now believe was to frighten me so much I wouldn't refuse. I was disgusted. I pushed past him while he yelled all sorts of abuse after me.' She looked around her but none of the other staff at the facility seemed to bat an eyelid and Johnny simply started laughing and joking again in another part of the yard. 'Not one of them looked my way or asked was I okay,' she explained. Was it a joke, albeit a sick one, she wondered? Later in the day she typed Creswell's name into Google, spelling it wrong once or twice, until she came across the newspaper articles featuring details of the Lyle case and the image of a younger Creswell on horseback.

That evening Sarah spoke to Ian about her shocking experience and what she had read when she googled him. Ian was also stunned, but the couple liked their new jobs and had literally packed up everything they had owned and taken a huge step to relocate to Northern Ireland. They decided to inform the stable owner, but, Sarah said, he simply shrugged his shoulders and it was left to Ian to confront Johnny. 'Creswell exploded in rage and after that the entire yard turned against us. We were completely ostracised. The power he held was ridiculous. I still don't know why people were obsessed with him. It made him untouchable,' she said. Unknown to Creswell, Ian had secretly recorded him as he salivated with rage. He had captured on tape the terrifying threats Creswell made, threats like: 'I'm gonna break your back and snap your neck and that cunt of a girlfriend of yours, she is gonna get what is coming to her too.'

Sarah and Ian had made their complaint and expected something to happen, but Johnny seemed untouchable and as far as they could see hadn't even been disciplined. They had shown their hand and now everyone was against them. After much discussion, and despite the commitment that they had made in moving to Northern Ireland and taking on new jobs in the first place, the pair packed their bags and returned to Scotland. After the New Year, when they had settled in new employment, they found themselves running over their experience with Johnny Creswell again and again. They simply couldn't believe what had occurred and that he had apparently got away with it while still enjoying the support of those around him. Sarah wondered how she would have fared out with Creswell if Ian hadn't been there watching out for her and she was sure there must have been others that had suffered the same treatment from him and who maybe hadn't had the backup that she had. His vicious threats to Ian that he would break his back had made it even worse. They had no doubt that he could have attempted to carry out his threats. They decided to go to the Scottish police and report in detail what he had said and done and they hoped that by going forward they would help someone else avoid a worse outcome than theirs.

In a detailed statement Sarah described the suddenness of Creswell's change and how he had rendered her speechless with his boasts about domestic abuse. She recalled every detail and told police about his claims about the shirt and how he had hoisted Abi up a tree in the woods while trying to hang her. Ian gave officers his phone containing the audio recording of Creswell threatening to 'snap his neck'. The couple told police that they felt they got no support in the yard and that the incident was treated as a mere falling out, a personality clash. This time, they were sure Creswell wouldn't get away with it. The complaint was passed on to the PSNI, who began their own investigation, but Creswell got word that he was going to be arrested and questioned about the indecent exposure and the threats to kill. Already avoiding cops over driving violations, he decided it was time to flee across the border and to his father, Herbie Lusby, with a story of persecution by the PSNI for crimes he hadn't committed. He was being hassled in Armagh, he told him, over tax and insurance issues on cars and for driving vehicles that weren't roadworthy. They were constantly stopping him and giving him grief and he needed to get offside so that he wouldn't lose his licence and be left unable to work.

Lusby was sympathetic to his son's predicament and had no reason to disbelieve his story. He'd grown up in Derry, a city that had been at the epicentre of the Troubles and where he had witnessed the worst of policing and politics. He'd followed his father into farming, buying up a large swathe of land on the city's west bank, where he'd grazed cattle in the late 1960s and throughout the 1970s. He'd watched a Catholic uprising that had started about housing conditions and resulted in civil rights marches where police beat campaigners with batons. By 1972 Derry was known throughout the world because of the Bloody Sunday massacre, when British soldiers had shot 26 unarmed civilians during a protest march in the Bogside area. Many of the victims had been shot while fleeing from the soldiers, the 1st Battalion of the Parachute Regiment, and some while attending to the injured. The march had been organised by the Northern Ireland Civil Rights Association to protest against internment without trial. Later, two investigations were held by the British government. Soon after the events the Widgery Tribunal largely cleared the soldiers and British authorities of any blame, but it was criticised as a 'whitewash'. Years later the Saville Inquiry, established in 1998, would conclude that the killings were 'unjustified' and 'unjustifiable'. While Lusby wasn't involved in the Troubles himself and wasn't political, he had sympathy for the people of Derry and their treatment by police and soldiers. He had seen how individuals could be downtrodden by the authorities and how corrupt police and politicians could be. Ironically, he'd got amazingly rich as a direct result of the greed and unfairness that had turned Derry into a war zone. A simple farmer, he'd been perfectly positioned when the landscape of the city changed and decades of human rights abuses created a map of change that turned his farmland into a goldmine.

He'd trousered his millions and moved to Porthall in Donegal, where he'd built a significant stud farm with plenty of accommodation. Apart from the main house, Port Hall, which he lived in, there were annexes and dormitories where staff and riders often slept. He'd dabbled in property acquisitions in Derry and even invested in a plan to set up boat trips along the River Foyle.

He'd helped set up the Donegal & Tyrone Farmers Hunt and attended their glamorous black tie balls. When his marriage ended he enjoyed a long relationship with a local woman and opened his vast home to family and friends. Lusby had never turned his back on his son, despite the complexities of his brief relationship with Johnny's mother, Donna, and in his time of need, with the police harassment he was allegedly suffering, Herbie agreed that he could come with Christina and stay in Donegal.

Lusby was popular in Porthall, as was his son Daniel. They'd developed pony schools, a breeding centre and showjumping facilities. The Lusbys were close and always welcoming to relatives from Derry, who were frequent visitors to Port Hall. From the beginning Creswell and Christina were embraced by the wider family. They moved into an annexe beside the property which was used by staff and it was agreed that they could help out on the stud farm and use Port Hall as a base to develop their own business until things calmed down. But the annexe quickly became cluttered and untidy, bins weren't emptied, dishes went unwashed and neither Johnny nor Christina was ever out of their mucky riding gear. Not long after their arrival, the visitors started to come; Jill Robinson, Hayley Robb and Katie Simpson. It soon emerged that Christina was pregnant with their first child. Creswell travelled over the border to work, dragging his horse box behind him; buying and selling, breaking in animals, riding out and teaching. Katie's visits often lasted over weekends and then stretched into weeks, and he often brought her with him, setting her to work too.

That December Christina gave birth to their first child, a girl they named Sandra after Johnny's grandmother. Katie soon began to stay even more and helped out with the new baby as well as working in yards in Derry and at Port Hall. While Herbie was initially reluctant for Creswell to bring another Simpson sister to his property, he had warmed to Katie, her skill with the horses and her work ethic. By then aged 16, she was a hard worker and hugely popular with the wider Lusby family. When she was rushed to hospital with a broken back after falling from a horse the family worried if they'd see her again. But despite being discharged to her mother's house for six months' recuperation, in no time she was back working in Donegal in a back brace, and by the end of that school year she'd finish her education for good to go to work full time with her sister and Johnny at Port Hall.

Johnny never told his father the true reason that he was lying low in Donegal. The PSNI would later say that they were 'actively' seeking him throughout 2016 and beyond. During a bail application years later the PSNI would say they had tried urgently to track him down to quiz him about the allegations made by Sarah and Ian, and they had issued an alert to police stations that he was wanted for an alleged sexual assault. Lists of what cars he could be driving and those associated with him were detailed, along with names of those he'd likely be in contact with. The PSNI would even claim they attended various events they thought he might attend, but he had foiled their every attempt, once fleeing with Christina in a car when he spotted them. However, in April 2017, as the PSNI continued to hunt for him, he was pictured in jockey silks in the winners' enclosure of the East Antrim point-to-point, not far from the area where the exposure incident happened. Months later, when they had had no luck tracking him down, the Public Prosecution Service (PPS) closed the case, directing no prosecution. Sarah received a letter stating that there was not enough evidence and the case was closed, but the information would be held on file. 'They don't believe me,' she said at the time.

By that time Christina was anxious to get back to work. She'd been on top form before the pregnancy, having clocked up three winners over 65 rides since 2014, mainly for Andy Oliver. But to start travelling to events again she needed her sister more than ever to help her with baby Sandra, and she knew she could rely on her. Katie's visits home became sporadic and when she did show up in Armagh she looked tired and thin and had little by way of money to show for her hard work in Donegal. She was embarrassed by her hands, calloused and torn from hard work, and she often tried to hide them in jumpers or in gloves. She also started asking people not to say that she had been home to visit. Her best friend Chloe and the Scott family worried for her, feeling she was being exploited by Johnny, but they had no idea what was really going on and how empowered he was becoming. In truth, he had created a dark world that was hidden in plain sight, and one from which Katie briefly escaped. Lying about her age, she had landed a job in a yard near Ayr in Scotland and on a weekend home got her sister Rebecca to drop her to the ferry. She told few people where she was going. For months she thrived at the yard and she was so popular that even on discovering that she was underage the owners agreed to keep her on. For that brief time Katie kept her own money and got to live a life free from the shackles and the demands of her sister's partner, a man who had all but taken over her life. She made friends and shopped for clothes and ate pizza and got days off. While she never revealed why she'd run away to Scotland, it was a brave leap for a young girl who'd never been away on her own and who had never left Ireland. Months into her adventure she booked a ticket home to see her mum and friend Chloe Scott. She looked well, rested and happy, but over the course of the week Christina and Johnny arrived to visit too. And just like that, Katie was back in Donegal, her brief sojourn in Scotland a fading memory.

At his father's stately home Johnny felt more powerful than ever before. Surrounded by land, wealth and women and having successfully evaded the law, he considered himself untouchable. Despite the filth of his living conditions, the increasingly chaotic state of his finances and the concern of many over his personal life, Johnny was on top of the world and carefully planning for his future. He was also growing his brood to make way for yet another young girl just a few years younger than Katie.

Rose De Montmorency Wright was a goofy-looking teenager, awkward and dishevelled, despite the upper-class background that her cumbersome name suggested. She was one of two sisters who lived in a country mansion outside Belfast with their parents, Jasper and Caroline De Montmorency Wright, who were both described by friends as horsey people. The De Montmorency Wrights were classic 'old money', born into privilege yet without the means of their ancestors. On her paternal side Rose could trace her blood back to the peerage of Ireland, and it was her grandmother, Jane Avril De Montmorency, who married Beverley John Rudyard Wright to give her the double-barrelled name she carried. The couple had reared Rose's father, Jasper, and their daughters, Caroline and Petronella, at the nineteenth-century Burnchurch House in County Kilkenny, which stood on forty acres and had a boating lake, where they were raised in quasi-Georgian splendour, fed with tales of Indian colonialists and African war heroes.

While not from any of the most famous big house families in Ireland, Jane De Montmorency was no less colourful than many of her rich peers. Before US President Barack Obama's 2011 visit to Ireland Jane had managed to trace her ancestry and was announced as his closest living Irish relative. With the help of a genealogical association and the US State Department, Jane had proved that she was a sixth cousin of Obama and discovered that their ancestors, the Kearneys, were the hereditary keepers of St Patrick's Crozier, an ancient relic of the patron saint of Ireland. The story made headlines across the world and turned the attention of the media on the elderly De Montmorency Wright matriarch. After her death in 2014 Jane's entire estate, the house and adjoining lands at Bennetsbridge, had sold for a mere €492,500 which, when divided three ways, made for a small inheritance for Jasper and his sisters. However, the sale a year later of the contents of her home and a collection of family heirlooms made the headlines when a late nineteenth-century poncho and war shirt with headdress and purse sold for €320,000 and put the history of the De Montmorency family, and their travels through Canada, America, India and Africa, into context. Jasper had met his wife-to-be Caroline at a social event in Derry during the late 1980s and the couple had settled in Newtownards, outside Belfast. They shared a love of horses and their two girls attended the prestigious Strathearn School, one of Northern Ireland's top grammar schools. Both Rose and Charlotte had been immersed in the North Down Pony Club since they were six years old and both became stalwarts of the club teams, entering competitions and championships across Northern Ireland and in the UK. In school they both landed a place on the senior showjumping team.

Rose was less academic than Charlotte. Severely dyslexic, she couldn't cope with studies and opted instead for a career in equestrianism, dropping out of school and working, initially unpaid, with horses. Johnny had met the De Montmorency Wrights at championships and was a regular visitor to their house for supper. Paintings of the De Montmorencys lined the walls, worthless but of sentimental value, and inherited from Burnchurch House along with tapestried sofas and ornate wooden cabinets that had once decorated elegant rooms but that now doubled as dog beds and shelves for piles of tack, reins, horse rugs, bridles and riding hats and boots, which were scattered everywhere. Johnny felt comfortable among the chaos and insisted to the De Montmorency Wrights that he could guide young Rose to achieve her potential. Along with Jill Robinson, Hayley Robb and Christina, and with Katie as a guiding hand, they would all help her improve in every way, he insisted. The 100-mile distance between East Belfast and his base in Donegal meant that Rose would have to stay over when she was training and so by 2017 she frequently joined the group at Port Hall, even attending a hunt ball at the Grianán Hotel, along with Katie, Creswell and Herbie, in February of that year, when she was just 16.

Herbie Lusby's seventieth birthday celebrations the following year were also an occasion for a huge family party, but at that point relations between Johnny, his dad and his half-brother Daniel had begun to sour. Apart from the growing number of young women who surrounded his son and who had been moved into Port Hall, Herbie worried that Johnny had set his sights on staying in Donegal more permanently. While he and Daniel had been more than welcoming and accommodating to him, they were growing concerned that Johnny was outstaying his welcome. It was nearly three years since he'd arrived on a temporary basis, seeking refuge from police attention for his driving offences, but now it was clear that he wanted part of Port Hall, which Herbie and Daniel had worked hard to build together. Johnny made no bones about the fact that he had set his sights on a parcel of land and an ambition to own and breed his own horses – a career where financial and business sense is as important as skill with the animals. And if Herbie Lusby knew anything, he knew that his son was bad with money, didn't like paying his bills and was living in a way that proved he was incapable of running a home. Bags of rubbish blocked the doorway to the annexe, the bathroom had never been cleaned and as far as anyone could see Johnny and his women lay down in the same clothing they worked in during the day. He tried to teach his son and encourage him to stay on top of things, but the creditors kept coming, owed money for labour, for feed or for odd jobs.

Johnny didn't see it as his fault when things went wrong. As far as he was concerned, it was elitist at the very top, where he wanted to be, and the business was populated by trainers and stud farm owners who had got a bit of a leg-up at the beginning. All his life he had worked for people who had inherited their family land or farms and transformed them into working studs and centres of excellence. Some had started small and worked up; others had inherited enough money to make it big from the get-go. Johnny had always been surrounded by both the haves and the have-nots. From the yards and stables surrounding his childhood home in Derry, where the wealthy were untouched by the violent riots and sectarianism that marked the lives of most, to Eglinton and Lenamore, the pony clubs and stables where he had learned his craft, built on lands passed down through generations and transformed from farms to equestrian centres. Caledon, Tynan and Glaslough, the three villages where he had come of age and honed his horsemanship, were dominated by the big houses that still provided employment for people like him. There were his employers, the doctor, the peeress and the wealthy horse owners whose colours he wore on his racing silks; his pony club pupils were largely privately schooled kids of middle-class parents; and he'd regularly felt he had to teach the horses he rode that they were not above him. Over the years Johnny might have been mistaken for one of the workers – a jockey, a stable hand, a groom – but he had always known what he really was. He'd known he was one of 'them', and in Donegal, at his father's palatial home, he had never felt nearer his dream. He might have once been seen as Herbie Lusby's less legitimate son, he may not have grown up at the manor, but he had finally got there and he was determined that he wasn't leaving without his birthright. He wanted land. And what Johnny Creswell wanted he took.

Five years his elder, Daniel Lusby was mild-mannered and pleasant. He loved farming, horses and hunting, but he was also well educated and took a more academic approach to stabling and training animals. Unlike his younger half-brother, he had been schooled in a classroom and not in the rougher ways of forcing horses to do his bidding. He also loved his family and was close to his cousin Paul Lusby, who was one of the most regular visitors from Derry. Paul too had warmly welcomed Johnny, Christina and their entourage, but he was also wary of Johnny and the way he spoke to his partner and young Katie. There were whispers in the yards about his peculiar habits and about the way they all lived together in filthy conditions. Some had noticed marks on Christina, but more so on Katie, slashes around her hands that looked like whip marks, but she never complained and only spoke gushingly about her life. Those who watched Johnny train them as they broke in horses found it extraordinary how high they would jump and the risks they appeared to take. The presence of Rose, who was so young, only added to the strange set-up.

But Johnny was well beyond caring what anybody thought of him. He'd managed to manoeuvre himself into the position of the head of a household where he could do whatever he wanted, and that included sex. Despite having a child with Christina and living with her, Johnny had numerous other sexual partners and would openly discuss where and who he was sleeping with. He'd proposition girls all the time within her hearing and often had encounters in stables as she stood waiting outside. For her part, Christina turned a blind eye or pretended not to notice, happy that no matter what she was his number one and the mother of his child. Apart from sex, his other focus was to get his business off the ground and by 2018 he was so serious about his plans that he had Christina register as a director of CJK Equine Limited, listing the company address as her mother's home in Middletown in County Armagh. While Johnny believed he was in charge of all aspects of his life, the finances needed to get an equestrian facility off the ground evaded him. He'd got work done at Port

Hall as he tried to forge a corner of the vast lands for his own use, but the bills would either be sent on to his father or wouldn't be paid. He worked the girls hard and long and they seemed to rarely sleep. He collected their wages and pocketed the money, but he was always in the red. He fell out with breeders, stableyard owners, farmers and trainers over unpaid debts or promises of money that never arrived.

In February 2019 the Donegal & Tyrone Farmers Hunt held its annual ball in Mount Errigal Hotel. Previously Johnny had attended social events with just Katie or Christina, but this time he would be the talk of the event. The only man at a table of eight young women, he looked like the cat who'd got the cream and posed happily for photographs surrounded by his female companions. In one snap he beams, red-cheeked, for the camera wearing an ill-fitting suit and crooked bow tie. On his left Christina wears a pastel pink off-the-shoulder gown, her long wavy red hair hanging loose down her back. She looks beautiful and happy and Johnny's arm is around her waist. To his right stands 18-year-old Rose De Montmorency Wright in a red off-the-shoulder dress with a plunging neckline, and black pointed shoes. Innocent and pale, she wears her hair up and has a simple silver chain around her neck. On closer inspection Johnny's hand can be seen inappropriately low on her waist. Beside her stands Katie in an all-encompassing gold and silver gown with an ornate Greek detail at the neck. Her auburn hair hangs in waves down her back. She is just 20 years old but she has a little over a year to live. Beside her, in the photograph, looking almost vixen-like and with heavy black smoky eye makeup is Hayley Robb. Her black hair falls to one side and her black ball gown slit reveals a slim leg and gold kitten-heel shoes. In other photographs Creswell shows an uncanny resemblance to his father – they both glow with rosy red cheeks. At a glance the photographs suggest happy times and a relaxed atmosphere between the women and Johnny, but underneath the smiles and the facade of normality things were unravelling at Port Hall. The announcement of Christina's second pregnancy and the imminent arrival of another baby didn't help.

Daniel and Herbie had broached the subject of Johnny's departure on a number of occasions, but each was left under no illusion that it would come at a price. He wanted land where he could develop his own equestrian centre and money for buying horses and equipment to start him off, he said. He would often mouth off about Lady Jane Alexander and how she had gone to war with her brother for her rights over their vast estate, a story that had hit the UK media when Lord Caledon was phoned for comment during a skiing holiday. The colourful Janey had died in May 2017, and her obituary in the *Irish Field* described how any animosity between the siblings had been well put to bed before she died.

For the past four years, Janey had been married to Turf Club and INHSC member Dr Fitz Gillespie and, in his oration, her brother, Lord Caledon, paid tribute to the great nursing care provided by Fitz to Janey who first fell ill before Christmas last year. To the surprise of many, he said that his sister had faced an uphill struggle from her birth in Switzerland as she was a 'Thalidomide baby' of the 1960s. Lord Caledon spoke of his sister's great fortitude, her positivity and kindness, how proud he was of her achievements in life and how happy she and Fitz had been since their marriage.

Things weren't to end up quite so friendly when it came to Johnny Creswell and his relatives. Johnny was clear in his demands. He wanted something suitable around Port Hall so that he could stay on at the house with all his women beside him. Herbie Lusby wanted to do right by his son but had become uncomfortable about Johnny's attitude and the lifestyle he led. Outsiders saw him as trying to take advantage of the generous Herbie and it was eventually Lusby who started to look towards Derry, a place he had plenty of investment property and which was just far enough away to restore peace and tranquillity to Port Hall.

By May 2019 Herbie Lusby had finally got rid of Johnny and his collection of women, four years after he'd arrived. A piece of land in Derry had been the lure, with the proviso that Johnny organise and pay for all his own legal papers and deeds of ownership, a detail that wasn't part of his unique skill set. Herbie had also agreed to have his name listed on a birth certificate issued at that time. It detailed the birth of Jonathan James Creswell in the district of Derry City and Strabane on 23 January 1988. His father was listed as Herbert Andrew Lusby, a farmer and his mother as Donna Elaine Creswell, a care worker from Briar Hill Gardens in Greysteel.

In Derry Johnny got to work immediately, hiring labourers to build a sand school and a gallops, but the bills were more than he had budgeted for and he never completed the legal necessities. He started to borrow money, turning as always to the women in his life to help. Katie Simpson managed to raise £10,000 for him from the credit union, and Hayley Robb would end up giving him £25,000.

By Christmas 2019 Christina was heavily pregnant with their second child. Two months later, when she gave birth, Johnny couldn't have been happier, posting on Facebook: 'Sandra has a baby brother born today at 4:30pm Christina Simpson doing good and baby 100 percent too.' The couple called the baby Michael. With a growing brood and struggling to finance his new business, Johnny was anxious to settle down, so he rented a home outside Derry for them all to live in. Gortnessy Meadows was situated in the townland of Lettershendoney, which was ironically advertised as being just a five-minute drive from Altnagelvin Hospital. A housing estate surrounded by rolling fields, it was billed as an exciting new location for first-time buyers and young families and it was there that Johnny found a small terraced townhouse with oil-fired central heating and measuring just 1,100 square feet. A hallway led to a living room to the front and a kitchen/diner to the back with a small downstairs toilet with room to hang a few coats. Upstairs he and Christina took the master bedroom, a small double with an ensuite shower room, while Katie and Rose shared the second small double. A single room was used for Sandra, while baby Michael remained in a cot. The house soon became cluttered with the outdoor gear and boots that everyone wore, dishes went unwashed and nobody cleaned up. But its location was perfect – near Johnny's mother Donna's home in Greysteel, which meant that she could help mind the children and Christina could get back to work.

Ever since it was built, Gortnessy Meadows had been populated by renters and often foreign workers doing labouring work around Derry and its townlands. It wasn't a neighbourhood in the traditional sense, but that suited Johnny and his peculiar lifestyle. By day he traded with farmers and breeders, he bought and sold animals, he was chased by debtors, and while he tried to develop his own parcel of land he rented out established indoor arenas to break and train the horses he hoped to sell. He was notoriously rough with horses and when they were finished they were simply bundled into the wagon sweating and dirty. In Derry he started to showjump again and take part in competitions. Christina and Katie were permanently at his side, and Rose too, but the girls rarely interacted with others and he did all the talking and negotiating, presenting himself as a family man. He spoke about Katie as if she was his daughter and at one point claimed he was going to buy her an expensive horse so he could further her career. 'He expected them to jump fences on young horses that weren't capable of it. They were always falling off and getting smashed to ribbons but they just got back on and went again. They were the roughest of the rough, always dirty, and the horses were never groomed,' one observer said:

You would wonder where their parents were and where did he find them but they were quiet and submissive and never interacted hugely with anyone but themselves. Then another young girl seemed to come on the scene and she was only a teenager but she seemed to be with them all the time and I do know she stayed at the house too. The mother had him on a pedestal and it was a case of whatever Johnny said went. The attitude was that he was the great 'Johnny Creswell'. But it was definitely weird. There were always showjumpers with girl followings, younger teenagers following them around wanting to groom and plait the horses but he was like a lion with his pride. There is an element of that in equestrian. When the riders are young and in the pony clubs it is more girls than boys but as they get older it gets tougher and rougher and the girls tend to fall away and then it's the men and they are treated like premiership footballers. They often go to events and they would be older men with young female grooms, sometimes from abroad. They are all-day events and they stay in the horse boxes and obviously there is a bit of this attitude that the men are rock stars. That is sort of accepted but with Johnny it was a step further than that.

Surrounded by the young women, Johnny's appetite for that stardom seemed insatiable and he was known for hunting out dark-haired women in stableyards. On Mondays, her day off, Hayley Robb would travel to Derry and meet with Creswell away from the other girls. At home at night he sometimes slept with Christina, but other nights he slept where he wanted. Rose was his 'queen' and his 'wee pet', while Katie had effectively become an unpaid labourer. Unknown to those outside the tight-knit circle he was sleeping with Katie too when he wanted, despite his relationship with her older sister.

For her part, Katie was changing as she matured, but she was terrified of Johnny, as were the other girls. Unbeknownst to most, Katie had been groomed by her sister's partner since she was ten years old to become his slave in every way. He had sex with her when he wanted, he beat and humiliated her regularly and he even collected her wages and gave her just a small amount of pocket money to survive. She'd tell friends that she was getting her 'bed and board' and had to work hard for it. But the figures didn't compute. At 21 she'd been controlled by Johnny for more than half her entire life and even when she had a bit of time off in the evenings she'd often have to babysit her niece and nephew or help get them to bed so Johnny and Christina could sleep. It wasn't much of a life, but she did enjoy competing across the country in showjumping and other equestrian events and she loved the horses, who seemed to keep her sane when she felt she might go crazy. Riding had also given her an outlet to meet people, albeit under the watchful eye of Johnny. She'd had a brief relationship in Donegal, but it was Derry where she'd fall in love.

CHAPTER 9

A DARK DAY

Katie knew Shane McCloskey liked her because of the way he would look at her, but she also knew that acting on that attraction, which was a two-way street, would be problematic for her on so many levels. Like the others, McCloskey had horses in his blood, had performed badly in school and by the age of 16 had dropped out and was working full time in the industry. He'd also had a long-term relationship with an older girl, who he'd gone into business with, which had ended in late 2019, and it was then that he set his sights on Katie. But his break-up meant he had a lot to untangle, and tensions were high. If the situation wasn't fraught enough, Johnny had done business with McCloskey's ex and knew her well. Katie didn't want any blame falling on her for the break-up and neither did she want to anger Johnny: after all, he might perceive that any hook-up she had could be damaging to his own business interests.

Johnny and how he might react was always foremost in Katie's mind. Over the previous two years he had become more and more demanding of her time, and both she and Christina had found themselves on the receiving end of his terrible temper more than once. In fact, over the previous two years Katie had been hospitalised 18 times with injuries from falls and from beatings. Each time, when Johnny took her to hospital he said she'd been in a horse-related accident. The horses, which Katie loved, he told admission staff, had kicked, trampled and thrown her, breaking her bones, giving her black eyes and bruising. Many of the 'falls' were nothing to do with the horses – sometimes it had been Johnny who'd head-butted her, whipped her or beaten her, just as he had Abi Lyle in the past. Christina had also suffered injuries, including a broken arm, but the birth of the children appeared to have secured her safety. Other injuries, however, were because of the style of training that Johnny demanded. Jumps would be raised impossibly high, circuits made incredibly difficult, and all the while Johnny would roar and whip both rider and horse in a terrifying regime which would often end in a tangle of hoofs and limbs. The girls would never complain or Johnny would fly into a black rage, demanding their phones, locking them in a room or in the stables or driving them furiously in his car.

For Katie, it was all she knew, having lived with Johnny since she was a young teenager, but unlike many of the horses that he had worked on, her spirit was still not broken. Katie still wanted to have a bit of fun and even a little bit of romance and there was nothing more normal than two young people who found one another attractive getting together. She flirted shyly with McCloskey whenever they saw one another and finally, over a weekend at the end of the summer, Katie had been brave. On Saturday 1 August she went for drinks with a friend in Moy and divulged to her during their evening that she'd started going out with Shane some weeks before. They were in the early stages of a relationship, she said, and in contact every day; and later that night they were due to meet up in her mother's house. Shane had stayed over in Middletown and the following morning the pair had risen early for work, around 5:30am, as Katie had an event to attend in Lurgan. Shane had set off on the quiet roads towards Derry. Katie sent him a text: 'I'm glad you came. Xxx,' she wrote. He replied with a red love heart and a short message: 'i am too xxxx'. But as he made his way through Omagh he spotted a familiar car and realised that he had been rumbled by a woman who suspected immediately that he was coming from a night with Katie. Earlier that morning, before 6am, and as McCloskey made his way to work, Creswell messaged Katie on Snapchat. At 5:49am he was angry that she hadn't replied and sent another message: 'U reply to my snap right fucking now'.

Anxious, Katie made her way to Jill Robinson's yard in Omagh to collect her horse. She met Rose and Johnny there, along with another young girl who had been spending time in the company of the group. Johnny travelled with Katie to Lurgan, quizzing her all the way. Katie knew what lay in store for her if Johnny found out what had happened the night before and started to delete messages between herself and McCloskey, getting worked up and worried very quickly. 'Johnny's asking me where you were last night. I've said I haven't spoken to you since the show . . . He'll probably ring you to see what you're doing this morning. She must have told him she seen you this morning. What are you going to tell him?' Shane responded: 'Katie is it not easier just to say the truth. This makes me look really bad.' But Katie replied: 'No way Shane. He'll go crazy. Please don't. Can you not say you were still in bed at the time. x' McCloskey responded: 'Why would he kill you. This is crazy. Like, fuck me, you're terrified of him. It's no good. Yes, I'll say I was in bed but he'll know I'm lying. I can't lie. Never could.'

As the day wore on the messages from Katie to Shane became increasingly panicked and she even asked him to send her a false narrative of messages as she knew Johnny would eventually scour her phone. That afternoon Johnny made contact with Shane and asked him where he had been the night before. Shane lied and said he'd stayed at his parents' house. Unknown to him, his cover had already been blown – someone had mentioned to Johnny that he'd been seen earlier that morning. It was an innocent conversation, a sliding doors moment, and the woman who spoke to Creswell could have had no idea how the idle chat would unleash a chain of events that would change countless lives for ever. She could have had no idea that lurking behind Creswell's facade of charming chancer and caregiver was a violent monster who was on the cusp of murder.

A panicked Shane tried to make contact again with Katie to update her on the situation, but to no avail. Following the event, Johnny decided that Rose would drive Katie's car and that she would travel in the back of the horse box with him as it was pulled along the roads back to Omagh to Jill Robinson's yard. From there he and Katie left on their own and made their way to Strabane. CCTV would later show Katie moving freely and trotting alongside a horse as it was being shown to a potential client. Then they got back into Johnny's car, at which point phone analytics would later trace their movements over the border to Lifford in County Donegal where they remained for 1 hour and 20 minutes before their phones started to ping again. They headed back into Northern Ireland towards an area called Claudy, outside Derry, where they stayed until after midnight. While officers could not say for sure where the phones were that night, there is a forest park just outside the village on the grounds of Cumber House, just like Castle Leslie, where he had taken Abi Lyle for a night of terror more than ten years before. Johnny still had control of Katie's phone and when a text came in at 11:17pm from innocent McCloskey wondering if he had done something wrong, he knew that his suspicions about their liaison were founded. Shane had texted, 'I don't know what I just wish u could said I didn't drive hour and half to sleep with u if that's what u thought i drove up just to see u cuse I really wanted this to work. I'm sorry.'

After midnight both Katie and Johnny's phones pinged back at Gortnessy Meadows. Rose would later tell police that she was at the house when they returned and that Katie had told her that she had been trampled by Nelson when she let him into a field. The next few hours would prove difficult to unravel. At 7:19am Shane texted Katie hoping she was okay, and he tried to call around 7:45am, but there was no answer.

At 7:52am Creswell left the house and both his phone and Katie's phone travelled to Greysteel, where he dropped off his children to his mother and then made his way back to the house. While Katie could not have been in the car, he had clearly taken her mobile with him. On the way back, at around 8:10am he rang Hayley Robb, who was on the way to meet Creswell. He was still on the phone with her when he returned to the house at 8:20am. As he unlocked the front door and walked in he suddenly started screaming, telling Hayley that he had just found Katie hanging from the stairwell. 'Ring an ambulance!' he shouted down the phone. Hayley frantically did so. She was still 40 minutes away and unsure what had gone on, but on the 999 call she told the operator that a young woman had been hanged in a house outside Derry.

'What is the address?'

'It's Gortnessy Meadows and there is a black Peugeot 207 outside.' Breathlessly, Hayley told the operator that she had received a call from a man at the house – Johnny Creswell.

'Is there anybody there? Do you have a number?'

Hayley read out Creswell's number and repeated that she was about 40 minutes away from the scene herself. Police at Derry's Strand Road Station were looped in to the call, but in the meantime Creswell had taken matters into his own hands and as the ambulance handler tried to reach him on the number they had been given he was already in the car with Katie slumped in the passenger seat. His phone was called repeatedly until he eventually picked up at 8:25am.

For six minutes the paramedics stayed on the phone with Creswell. First they tried to establish his exact location.

'You are on the way to the hospital?'

'Yes,' he said. 'On the way to Altnagelvin Hospital.' He said the patient was in the car with him, adding: 'I thought she was breathing but I don't think she is breathing.' Even during the call Creswell managed to refer to the operator as 'darling' as he told her that Katie was only 20 years old. Then the handler told him he'd have to stop the car and try to help Katie.

'Okay. Okay. If you could pull over,' the voice said.

'I'm driving,' came the panicked response. Eventually Creswell pulled over the car and the call handler instructed him how to carry out CPR on Katie. 'They will come to me?' he asked about the ambulance. The call handler spoke reassuringly to Creswell, asking him to count out his reps to make sure he was doing the right rhythm.

'Just count out one, two, three, four for me just so I know that you are doing the right rhythm,' she said.

At 8:28 Creswell was counting out his CPR reps down the phone as the ambulance raced to meet him. The call handler told Creswell where to position his hands, counting out 'One, two, three, four' in a steady rhythm. Creswell counted too, breathlessly saying down the phone: 'The poor girl. Poor wee darling. She's only twenty . . . Ah, no, Katie, darling . . . I think I'm hurting her.' He counted again, then said, 'Ah, my God. There's nothing happening here. Nothing.' It would later be discovered that while Creswell was supposed to be trying to keep Katie alive, using both hands, he was in fact switching her phone to airplane mode so that it couldn't be tracked.

The paramedic response car arrived shortly before the ambulance and took over. In the background of the 999 call, ambulance sirens are eventually heard in the distance, getting louder as help approached. The first responders would later recall how they arrived to find Katie in the passenger seat wearing a collared T-shirt and underwear but nothing else. The shirt would turn out to be the one she had worn at the equestrian event the day before. They also noted she had only faint marks on her neck, which were not overly deep. They also noticed that she had bruises on her lower legs.

'I just came back and she was hung,' Creswell told them, detailing how she'd been hanging by a black cord from the bannisters. He claimed he'd cut the cord and attempted CPR before moving her into the back of his car and making his way towards the hospital. She was unconscious, her heart had stopped beating and she was not breathing, but as the paramedics worked on her they managed to restart her heart and rushed her to Altnagelvin and its A&E department. On the roadside a PSNI officer who had accompanied the first responders interviewed a sweating Creswell and asked him his name and what relationship he had with Katie. 'She is like my wee sister-in-law,' he responded.

'What is her name?' the officer asked.

'Katie Simpson. She is twenty-one. She is the best wee girl.'

Asked what had occurred, he said that he had found Katie hanging that morning. While her home address was Armagh, he said that she was staying in Gortnessy Meadows. 'We just moved into it not that long ago. Number 5 Gortnessy or number 4 Gortnessy. That is where it happened,' he said. But Creswell had given the wrong house number – they were actually living at number 81. He also told officers that Katie did not have a mobile phone.

As the ambulance made its way to the hospital, Creswell was instructed by police to follow. When he did arrive he was with Hayley Robb in her Ford Fiesta and he was wearing a different top. Outside the hospital, police spoke with Hayley. They were aware that she had had a very traumatic morning, but they needed to try to establish what happened. 'I left my house at seven-thirty this morning in Banbridge and coming up through Moneymore coz it's the quickest way. I was chatting on the phone and Johnny rings and he was roaring and he is like "Ring an ambulance."'

'He phoned you?' the officer asked, trying to establish how it was Hayley who had ended up making the 999 call.

'I was on the way there anyway. I was going to clip the horses. I was like, what is wrong? He said Katie had tried to hang herself and I was like "fuck" and I rang straight away and got them eventually and rang him and said make sure you answer the phone because they are calling on a random number. I was still half an hour away, the other side of Dungiven. When I got there the ambulance had already taken her away. He literally came out and we went to the hospital.'

The police wondered what Creswell had said in the car to the hospital. 'When you picked him up and took him there did he say what happened?'

'No, he just said I don't know why she had done this or nothing,' she replied.

Confused by the comings and goings at the house and the timeline of the morning, the police officer looked at Hayley and asked her directly, 'What is your relationship?'

'We are friends,' she replied. 'And I'm friendly with all of them. They are all horsey people and they were at a show in the Meadows yesterday and they were in great form. I was coming up to clip the horse. I come up every Monday on my day off.' But she stopped there. There was no way Hayley Robb was going to say any more about her bizarre relationship with Creswell or any of the women to any officer. Theirs was a secret club, a world which only concerned them and one where Creswell ruled supreme.

Police then spoke again with Creswell and he told them he had left his home that morning to drop his kids off. He made a point of saying that he had said goodbye to Katie, as had his three-year-old child. He said he hadn't come straight to the hospital – he had gone home because his friend Hayley wouldn't have known where he was. Asked if Katie had any partner in her life, he said she hadn't.

At Altnagelvin medical staff had hooked Katie up to a life support system in its intensive care unit. They had noticed the bruising on her body, but Creswell told them that she had fallen from a horse the day before. Doctors noted that she had bruises on her thigh, calf, right forearm and right and left hands. She had grazing on her foot and red marks on her neck. She also had a cut to the right of her lip and appeared to have vaginal bleeding. One month into the Covid pandemic, the hospital was in lockdown, with all visits fiercely controlled for the safety of patients and the health service. But this was a special case, a 21-year-old girl clinging to life after a suspected suicide attempt. Her family would have to be allowed at her bedside if she had any hope of recovering, but the most important investigation was around brain activity. As the morning wore on Noeleen arrived, and Rebecca too, and both whispered reassurances to Katie that she was going to be okay. Creswell and Christina were there too. Rebecca later recalled asking him about her sister's phone, but he said it had likely fallen in the panic when she was being transferred into the ambulance. At some point he and Christina left the hospital but they returned later in the day.

Meanwhile, police visited Gortnessy Meadows to make some standard checks around Katie's admission to hospital. They checked their systems for Jonathan Creswell and found that he had a few traffic offences, but nothing that would red-flag him. It was one of the many incredible aspects of the case that both his previous conviction for the assault of Abi Lyle and the complaint made against him by Sarah in Antrim failed to show up. Both had somehow been buried in the system. In the house officers videoed the scene, observed and secured the noose and then left.

Across the equestrian world, word was spreading fast about what had happened to Katie. The news that she had attempted to take her own life was greeted with shock and disbelief. Most knew Katie as a happy girl who had never had suicidal ideation, had not suffered from depression or mental health difficulties and who was on a career path to greatness in the saddle. She was pretty and bubbly and kind and hardworking and she had plans. Her best friend, Chloe Scott, was absolutely devastated, but because of Covid restrictions she couldn't rush to the hospital where Katie was clinging to life. She picked up as much detail as she could about what had happened but she could feel the hairs on her neck begin to rise. Not because she believed her friend had been in such a dark place that she had chosen to end her own life. Instead, the shadowy figure of Jonathan Creswell over-whelmed Chloe's thoughts. She'd heard it was Creswell who'd found Katie and that he had brought her to hospital. Chloe had never liked Creswell and she suspected that he had been less than kind to Katie in the past, working her like a slave and taking her money. She knew he was bad and now she couldn't get him out of her mind, nor could she believe her friend was capable of suicide. Later that day Jill Robinson arrived at the hospital and she, along with Hayley and Johnny, went for a drive.

The following day Tanya Fowles was at home in Tynan when her phone rang. A long-term friend in a distressed state was calling with the news that Katie Simpson, a young girl from their village, was clinging to life in Altnagelvin Hospital, having attempted to hang herself, something which Tanya's friend simply couldn't believe. 'Gosh, that is terrible,' Tanya said. 'I think I know the girl you're talking about. I've seen her at shows.' Just like Chloe, Tanya's friend was concerned that something wasn't quite right with the story she had been told. While it isn't uncommon for people who hear about suicides to be in a state of disbelief, Tanya could hear panic in her friend's voice as she started to tell her about Katie.

Katie had been living with her sister Christina and her partner in Donegal, her friend said, and more recently in Derry, and working in their horse training business. Tanya did her best to console her friend and she listened carefully, wondering if there was anything she could or should do to help. This man had been working Katie hard, her friend told her, more than 12 hours a day, and had been pocketing her money. She was like an unpaid worker and they had hardly seen her of late as she had less and less time to do anything with friends or family. It did strike Tanya that poor Katie was being exploited, in that she was working for free, but as her friend chatted about Katie's partner she dropped into the conversation how he had previously lived in Caledon and had once threatened a former partner with a bath of bleach. All of a sudden Tanya was all ears. 'What? Jonathan Creswell?' She asked her friend, her blood beginning to run cold and the hairs on her neck standing on end.

Tanya's mind began to spin. She had covered the Abi Lyle case in her role as a journalist in Dungannon Magistrates Court and later in Dungannon Crown Court, and had been present at every hearing. She remembered writing extensively about the case. She knew the domestic violence officer PC Nuala Lappin, who had dealt with Creswell at the time, she remembered the details of the attempted strangulation, the hanging, the violence. She knew in her heart and soul that Jonathan Creswell should be nowhere near women, that he was a domestic abuser of the worst kind, and that questions needed to be asked about Katie's hospital admission. After putting down the phone, Tanya dialled Nuala's number and together they talked about the scenario, both agreeing that the issues should be flagged with police in the event that they didn't know the calibre of individual they were dealing with in Creswell.

Tanya rang another officer she knew from covering the courts and explained her concerns, and then she made contact with Strand Road PSNI station, the station that covered Altnagelvin and its surrounds. She was given the name of a sergeant to speak to about the case and when she did she gave a brief outline of her own background and told him about the conversation she had had with her friend that morning. She told the officer that she expected that police already knew all about Creswell but just in case she wanted to highlight his history with domestic abuse and strangulation. She was told the investigating officer was on leave but that she would contact her on her return. At some point on the Thursday of that week, Tanya missed a call on her phone. A woman left a voicemail, but when Tanya rang back a male voice asked callers to leave a message. She left a message to say she was available.

At the same time a friend of Katie's was also trying to contact police to red-flag Creswell and his possible involvement. In the hospital Christina and Rebecca were at Katie's bedside as often as they were allowed, along with Noeleen, but Creswell kept up a vigil outside the room and was allowed in to visit her in intensive care, despite not being a relative and despite the strict Covid protocols that were in place. Medical staff would later note their concerns about his behaviour and how he appeared to remain vigilant around her when friends were invited to go and spend time with her. He would kiss her and tell her he loved her as she lay in her hospital bed and seemed to be the one most invested in her condition. Aunts, uncles and even her grandparents were forced to conduct video calls with her as they encouraged her to get better and to fight for her life. Creswell told her family that, while he didn't believe in God, he was praying for Katie.

Tanya Fowles had still heard nothing back from police or the number she had tried to call. 'On Saturday the eighth of August at eleven-thirty a.m. I had sent a text, a kind of a reminder, you know . . . Sorry I missed your call. Can I ring you later today or whenever suits.' But there was no response.

Six days after the ventilator had tried to pump life back into her young body, Katie suffered a massive cardiac arrest in hospital. Her family were called in and told the terrible news. They were allowed one last moment with her as she drew her last breath. At her bedside was Noeleen, Rebecca, Christina and Johnny Creswell, who would later take to Facebook to tell his followers and friends of his grief. 'One of the best friends i could ever ask for,' he wrote; 'one of the most talented horse women i ever met . . . best hunting buddy i the world . . . fearless in the saddle . . . fearless across the country . . . hardest worker born . . . best aunty to my two children, Sandra, Michael Christina Simpson myself and the word are going to struggle without you beautiful . . . we love you so much . . . can't wait to see you again.'

Early that morning Tanya Fowles had sent a message to the same number at 9:49am. It read simply, 'Katie passed away early this morning.'

Two days later Tanya was still waiting for a call back from Derry police so she contacted a detective she knew from covering the case of Charlotte Murray at Dungannon Magistrates Court, an extraordinary trial that had been the first of its kind in Northern Ireland and that had just recently concluded with John Patrick Miller being found guilty of Murray's murder. Miller was the former partner of Murray, a 34-year-old woman who had disappeared in 2012 and whose body had never been found. The trial had lasted over a month. Miller had denied having anything to do with her murder, saying he believed she was still alive and he hoped she would some day 'walk in the door and say sorry for all this'. However, detectives had told the court that the couple had worked together and been engaged but that things went sour months before she went missing in October 2012. She had spent a night with another man and Miller had received intimate images of his fiancée. Around the time of her disappearance he had gone online searching for pawn shops where he could sell an engagement ring. He'd tried to cover up her disappearance. A post had appeared on her Facebook account, saying: 'I'm so p***ed off with life. I have to go away for a while.' A text was also sent from her mobile phone to her new employers saying she wouldn't be coming in. Police and the jury believed that the phone was in Miller's possession at the time. There had been evidence of an earlier abusive relationship and an ex-partner had said he'd knocked her down the stairs. The home search proved vital; traces of Charlotte's blood were found in the bathroom of the house and on the wall behind the toilet.

Just like the Creswell case, Tanya had been at every hearing and had built up a rapport with one of the lead detectives on the Murray murder squad. Like others, she was becoming increasingly concerned that Creswell might have been responsible for Katie's death and that it wasn't a suicide. She'd been gathering what details she could and had pieced together a picture of the life Katie had with Creswell and the bizarre life he led, surrounded by women who all seemed to be in some sort of a relationship with him. She had pored over her notes from the Lyle trial and underlined certain aspects of it: the crossing of the border, the use of ligatures, the jealousy, the violence and the support of the women around him. 'I think he killed Katie. I don't think it was suicide at all,' Tanya said. The detective listened to her concerns and said he would try to find out what was happening in Derry.

Tanya had no idea that staff at the hospital had been concerned too by Katie's injuries; her bruises and vaginal bleeding. While the police systems had somehow hidden Creswell's more serious offences, by simply googling his name anyone could find newspaper articles from 2010 about the attack on Abi Lyle. The journalist was also unaware that while Katie was still alive one nurse had visited Strand Road police station to air her concerns and to try to get officers to treat Creswell as a suspect. Police officers had taken notes but hadn't asked her for a statement. Like others who were raising concerns, she believed that they were already investigating her death as suspicious.

Unknown to both Tanya and the nurse there was another person who was concerned about what had happened to Katie.

Paul Lusby simply couldn't believe the story about suicide. In fact, knowing Katie as such a positive and happy person, he found it incomprehensible from the start that Katie would take her own life. Paul had been contacted by Christina to tell him Katie had attempted suicide and was in intensive care in hospital. She had told him she didn't want him to hear the news through social media. Paul had gone to see Donna, Creswell's mother, who he'd later say seemed more concerned about the effects of the suicide on Johnny and Christina than about Katie. She had told him her son's phone was out of action, so if he wanted to check in he'd have to call Christina. Lusby next headed for Gortnessy Meadows to see if there was anything he could do. He later told police in a statement that when he went there Hayley Robb came out of the house to greet him. He said that Shane McCloskey was there too and that he'd made some small talk with them. Hayley, he said, told him that Johnny and Christina were asleep upstairs and that the suicide was planned. She told him, he said, that Katie had been in good form and had gone out with friends in Armagh the previous Saturday but had called in with an elderly neighbour and made some cryptic comment about seeing them soon, insinuating they would both be dead. He also said that Hayley told him Katie had called in to work sick on the Monday morning and had gone back to bed. She said she'd listened as Creswell got the kids ready to leave the house and had given the children a big hug. When Creswell returned, she recounted, Katie was hanging. Lusby told police that, to him, the story didn't add up. On Wednesday 5 August, he tried ringing Chrstina, but she didn't answer, so he called Jill Robinson. In a statement, he would later claim that Jill also told him the suicide was planned months in advance and that Katie had twice deliberately crashed her car, hitting a central barrier on the motorway the first time and then driving into a lamppost on another occasion. He said Jill told him that a friend of hers who was a bereavement counsellor said these actions were classic for someone with suicidal ideation.

When he wasn't at Katie's bedside Creswell was spreading the news of how unwell she had been. He met with Shane McCloskey and told him of having found her hanging, advising him not to tell anyone that he was seeing Katie. He told another man that Katie had planned her suicide and had even tried to kill herself the previous Saturday night, when she was staying with her mother in Armagh, and had left a mark on the banister. He told that man a different story about what had happened when he went to go to his mother's house with the children that morning, saying that Katie had come downstairs and given the children a kiss. He said he'd stopped off at a shop on the way back to the house to buy Hayley and Katie some breakfast. He claimed that he had seen on Katie's phone how she had looked up how to do a hangman's noose and found other straps in her bag that she had planned to use. He said he hadn't been able to get through to the ambulance service as he'd no phone coverage.

Katie Simpson died at 3:17am on the morning of 10 August from a cardiac arrest caused by the brain injury she had sustained when her airways had been cut off. Again the news travelled fast. Paul Lusby later said that it was Jill who had phoned him to break the news. During the week Katie was in hospital Lusby had been so convinced that something was not right that he'd contacted the anonymous website Crimestoppers to report his suspicions about what had happened to her, naming his cousin

Jonathan Creswell as possibly having played a role in Katie's death. After she died, Lusby contacted Crimestoppers again to say he was highly suspicious of Creswell and uncomfortable about his entire story. A discussion he'd had with Creswell about Katie had come to an abrupt end, he said, when Paul had aired his feelings around her 'suicide'. Blushing with anger, Creswell had taken out a book of pictures of her showjumping and closed down any more conversation about her.

A day after her death a post-mortem took place at the hospital, by which time the injuries noted by staff on her admission had faded. A detective from Derry CID was present during the pathology examination, during which Creswell's version of events was discussed. He had said she'd been trampled by a horse, a 16-hand giant called Nelson, and his story had been backed up by Rose De Montmorency Wright. Neither the police officer nor the pathologist were aware of what was going on in the background and that an intricate cover-up had begun. In a police log a detective made an entry that the pathologist had asked why the case was being look at so closely and that the officer present had said there was 'a degree of suspicion' around it. A police officer would also later tell the Ombudsman that the pathologist concluded that cause of death was 'probably hanging', but then amended it to 'possible hanging'. Whatever the specific language, the CID later concluded that the case of Katie Simpson's death was not suspicious and returned it to the uniformed detectives that night as a suicide. 'They take one day to look into this matter with all the concerns that were there. One day!' says Tanya Fowles.

From the moment Katie's body was returned to her mother's house in Middletown on Wednesday 12 August, Johnny Creswell took charge of the proceedings. As those from the equestrian world came in their droves to say their goodbyes to the talented showjumper and to pay their respects to her family, Creswell presented himself as chief mourner, standing over the coffin and repeatedly petting Katie's head. He commented that she looked well and made a joke that her hair was brushed for the first time in a long while. For two days the guests came to wake her body, laid out in an upstairs bedroom and dressed in her hunting jacket. They sympathised with the family members and shook Creswell's hand too. At the house, on the morning of the funeral, he ordered everyone to show up in hunting gear to honour her memory. Her mother Noeleen would later say she overheard him whisper 'sorry' to Katie and touch her arm before the coffin was closed. And he was among those, along with Rose, who carried her to her grave. Some of those looking on didn't believe his grief was real. Later, Katie's aunt, Paula Mullan, went with her partner, Jimmy, to Strand Road police station and reported at the desk that they didn't believe Katie's death was a suicide and that they believed she might have been murdered by Creswell. The couple were told that their suspicions would be passed on.

Tanya Fowles was at Katie's funeral too, watching with growing suspicion what she later described as an Oscar-winning performance from Creswell.

I remember he had a black jacket on. Once Katie was on the ground his attitude was let's all go up Main Street and go to the pub. He didn't drink but it was like it was all over and done with, finished, move on. The alarm bells were there for me and for me it wasn't even guesswork that he

144

had an involvement, it was a fact. I was literally there at the graveyard waiting to hear the sirens. I thought they were coming to arrest him but nobody came and the funeral was over.

Tanya began to dig further into the facts of the case. She'd heard that Katie's phone was missing, and her laptop. She remembered that Creswell was obsessed with phones and recalled how he had taken Abi Lyle's phones and smashed them up. Had he done the same with Katie's? On 19 August, two weeks after Katie was taken to hospital, Creswell was spoken to again by police and provided a similar account to that given at the hospital, which had been recorded on body cam footage. He said he'd had a good relationship with Katie but made no reference to her romance with Shane McCloskey.

Two weeks after the funeral Paul Lusby offered to help Creswell and Christina clean out the rental house at Gortnessy Meadows, as they had to return it to the letting agency. He was increasingly worried about the behaviour of everyone around Katie's death and from the very beginning had been sceptical. He later described how, when he went to the house to help clean up, he saw a letter from the estate agent about unacceptable behaviour somewhere in the house and believed it to be a type of eviction notice. He told police that he met Rose and chatted with her, telling her he'd heard that Shane had stayed with Katie a few nights before her death, but Rose denied it, saying the last person to ask Katie on a date was another guy and that she had 'asked Johnny to go with her'. Lusby found the story strange, particularly as during the funeral Johnny had remarked, about Rose, 'If she had committed suicide I'd have not even been surprised because of the way I've been treating her, but Katie?'

Lusby said he helped Christina clean up and as he was vacuuming the upstairs of the house he noticed spots of blood on the master bedroom door. He described the blood as 'light splashes, low down on the door'. He said he showed them to Christina who, he claimed, replied: 'Jeepers, I don't know what that is. There shouldn't be blood.' He said Christina had a cloth and used it to wipe the blood away, also wiping fingerprints off the wall. Two or three steps from the bottom of the stairs, he claimed, she said to him, 'Have you seen this?' He told police she was referring to a piece of wood with a smudge on it and Christina told him that was where Katie's head was and where she was hanging. Christina, he said, then put her head in the place where the mark was and said all Katie would have to do was stand up. He described Christina as 'looking puzzled'. He told officers he asked her about the rope and Christina said it was tied up over the banister. 'I went back up the stairs to have a look but I couldn't see marks, abrasions or scuffs,' he would say. 'There were no signs of anything being tied to that banister.' After they finished cleaning Christina asked him to have the remaining oil in the tank returned to her. Later he picked up the phone and dialled the police non-emergency number, asking to speak to the officer in charge of the investigation. He was told someone would contact him but nobody did, so he called again. Again, he got no response.

As September arrived, Creswell's life started to return to some normality and he got back to work buying and selling horses. After leaving Gortnessy he and Christina had moved in with his mother in Greysteel. Her house was already cluttered and in disarray, but with their arrival things only got worse. Johnny's finances were still in a mess and he was always looking for opportunities to beg, steal or borrow money. Unknown to many he had managed to take Katie's bank card and cleared what he could of her account as she had lain dying in hospital. He'd also tried to tap her mother Noeleen for a loan as she sat at her daughter's bedside. Christina, on the other hand, was feeling charitable and had posted a birthday fundraiser for Pieta House, a suicide awareness and counselling service, on her Facebook page. Jill Robinson, among others, donated to the cause.

But while life was getting back to normal for some, those who were trying to get the attention of the police weren't happy that they were being ignored. As the weeks wore on, the nurse from the hospital was back at the police station, concerned that they were not investigating matters around Katie's death, but she was assured they were following it up. Extraordinarily, members of Katie's own family were also concerned, including her mother Noeleen, who was beginning to ask questions too. Devastated with grief, she rang police saying she couldn't understand how any young girl would kill themselves in just a T-shirt and underwear.

In the background local officers were preparing a file for the coroner for an inquest into Katie's death and were carrying out some interviews. On 10 October Rose was asked for a witness statement. In it she said she believed that Katie had planned her suicide, having previously attempted to take her own life. She claimed that on the Sunday night after the Lurgan show, when she had returned home with Johnny Creswell she had spoken to

Katie and that Katie had told her about being trampled by a horse. She claimed that Katie had laughed about it and rolled her eyes before going to bed. The next morning, she said, she had got up and made tea for Katie and Johnny before heading to work, claiming that Katie had told her she was taking the day off, which was unusual.

Also in October, two months after Katie's death, Paul Lusby was asked to meet with a detective at Derry's Strand Road station. He told them everything he knew but while they didn't take a statement they did make notes and Paul left convinced that something would finally break in the case. Weeks later, again concerned that nothing had happened, he contacted police again and was told they were satisfied that nothing untoward had happened. In the background Tanya Fowles was getting more and more annoyed at being stonewalled by the police. In one conversation, when she was attempting to pass on what she knew about Creswell she was asked how she had such detailed information about him. She told the officer she had covered the case in court. 'It was like, oh, you're a journalist. You should call the press office. I couldn't believe it.'

Tanya knew one thing for sure. She'd need to keep a record of everything and would have to start agitating the authorities by using the official communication channels that they wanted her to. On 22 November she sat down to write to the PSNI's News and Media Desk, or the press office, to log her concerns. She knew now that she needed to file all her complaints and all the responses she received. 'In respect of the admission of 22-year-old Katie Simpson to Altnagelvin Hospital on 2 August as a result of an alleged suicide attempt followed by her death in ICU on 9 August we have received a number of reports around the police investigation,' she wrote.

Some of these make very serious allegations around concerns reported to police in the afternoon of Miss Simpson's death but little heed has been paid to the same. These persons do not believe this matter is being treated with the serious-ness they feel it deserves. We are aware of all names involved including whom they identify as a suspect. The individual in question is known to have a very relevant record and indeed I am aware of this as I covered it in full at the time. There are stark similarities. It has also emerged that this individual was not appropriately flagged on the relevant risk register at the time around a propensity for violence toward women.

We are also aware of a report to police after Miss Simpson's death pointing towards potential injuries on admission to hospital attributed [to] an equestrian incident the day before her admission to hospital. The person who made this call was the same person who gave a defence statement for the individual in the previous case, consenting the victim was unstable, had caused injuries to herself and her attacker was entirely innocent. He later pleaded guilty to all with two exceptions (choking the victim and destroying her phone, which were left on the books). Taking this from the perspec-tive of those who feel their concerns have been either ignored or trivialised, against the seriousness of the issue, we are compiling a copy.

Tanya got a simple response:

Police in Derry/Londonderry received a report of a sudden
death of a 21-year-old female at a hospital on 9th [10] August
2020. Our enquiries establish the circumstances surrounding
the death are continuing and as such it would not be appropriate to comment further at this time. Anyone with a complaint
regarding police actions should contact the police ombudsman.

That same month Paul Lusby, still unknown to Tanya, was
realising that he too needed to keep a better record of what was
happening about the concerns he was raising and his attempts to
alert the police to his suspicions. He applied through a subject
request order for the notes taken during his visits to police stations
and was told that they had been shredded. A sense of paranoia
began to set in.

On 4 December, Tanya wrote again about the CID involvement
when Katie was in ICU. She simply couldn't believe that they had
made a decision that Creswell's story was true without even
investigating it. 'On what date was a complaint received? On
what date was a decision taken? What was the outcome of a
PONI [Police Ombudsman for Northern Ireland] investigation?
Is any action to be taken against those who made the original
decision not to authorise CID involvement?' she wrote.

Her letter and the fact that it was clear the concerns about
Creswell and the story of Katie's suicide were growing rather
than abating had caused much discomfort in the PSNI. Finally,
before Christmas, a senior officer, Detective Superintendent Jason
Murphy, took a look at the case and decided that it would be

worth investigating the death of Katie Simpson with greater clarity. He knew there was something fishy about the case and in particular about the man at the centre of it, who was living as carefree a life as he always had. Within weeks, the case was removed from Derry and handed over to fresh investigators in Armagh, a team who would very quickly realise that Creswell had almost got away with murder.

CHAPTER 10

THE MURDER
INVESTIGATION

The opportunities missed by investigators in the immediate aftermath of Katie's supposed suicide attempt would ripple directly into the new murder probe. But while many decisions couldn't be undone, officers knew they had to build a circumstantial case against Creswell, one that would directly challenge his version of events, and they quickly started to bring in teams of experts who could discredit his story. Meteorologists, pathologists, bruise definition experts and even hanging experts were called upon and asked for lengthy reports on the facts of the case to forestall any challenges he might take in his defence.

The post-mortem conducted at the hospital after her death was revisited and the pathologist reviewed pictures identifying bruises on Katie's limbs that showed patterning like horizontal linear bands of purple bruising. In places the bruises were parallel and suggested that she had been struck with a rod-like instrument. A senior forensic pathologist brought in to re-examine the available evidence said that he believed that Katie had been assaulted with a weapon prior to suffering a cardiac arrest. He could not be exact on a timeline.

The pathologist, from looking at the marks on her neck, said it was not possible to rule out suicide by hanging, but he would have to look at other evidence to consider whether the hanging might have been staged. First, he looked at the marks and concluded that they were not consistent with the characteristics of the ligature that Creswell said he had found around Katie's neck. Injuries to the backs of her hands, he said, were likely defensive ones as she tried to fend off blows during the assault. He noted there were grip-type marks on the back of her right thigh, which, he believed, were consistent with a sexual assault. The injuries to her face, right forearm, shin, knee and thigh, he told police, strongly suggested she had been assaulted during an attack that had likely lasted many hours.

Armed with the pathologist's suspicions over the ligature, police gathered evidence from the stairwell in a further bid to disprove Creswell's story. The Crown would make the case that she was never in the position that he claimed she was. One by one, the experts brought in had all agreed with the PPS case that Creswell had told lies and made up a scientifically incredible story. Police had simulated suspension from the same bannisters that Katie was supposed to have hung herself from and had discovered they could hold no more than four stone – a far cry from the 11 stone Katie weighed when she died. The ligature had been examined for drop length, which also didn't match up with what Creswell had told police. Very quickly it became clear that Creswell had crudely staged the suicide and that nothing he said added up. The police were, however, still on the back foot because of so much that had been missed in the immediate aftermath of Katie's arrival at Altnagelvin

Hospital. And as yet, they had no idea that there were people in the background helping Creswell with a cover-up.

Mopping up what they could in terms of statements from witnesses and those who should have been spoken to at the time of Katie's death, the PSNI team gathered their case. In January 2021 they went back to Rose, who now said that Katie had fallen from a horse and that she had witnessed it. She claimed that Katie had hurt her jaw but didn't complain or mention it. In a second statement she told police that she had met with Hayley Robb a few days after Katie was brought to hospital. She said that Robb had told her she'd cleaned blood from around the stairs in the house at Gortnessy. Looking at photos of the house taken after Katie had been taken to hospital she also said that she could see Katie's phone at the side of her bed – an impossibility, since by then officers knew that Creswell had had Katie's phone and had disposed of it in a field. In a final statement she said she'd been living in the house at Gortnessy for six months and repeated her claims about talking to Katie and bringing her tea.

The PSNI had also gone back to some of those who had tried repeatedly to raise their concerns but who had never been asked for statements. They contacted the nurse from the hospital and she gave a statement; and in February, six months after he had first tried to raise awareness of his suspicions, Paul Lusby gave a three-page account to police recalling how he had heard of Katie's death and the various conversations he had had with Hayley Robb, Jill Robinson and Rose De Montmorency Wright in relation to Katie's so-called suicidal mindset and the sequence of events on the night in question.

Paul described how he had first met Katie five years before at his uncle Herbie's farm in Porthall, where she was working with horses along with her sister Christina and Johnny Creswell, his estranged half cousin. He told officers that Katie was there quite a lot and subsequently all the time. He described her as a really pleasant girl who was quiet and who smiled a lot and was always in good form. He detailed how before her death Katie had lived at Gortnessy Meadows with Christina and Creswell and their kids, along with Rose. The adults, he said, were all involved in horse jumping and tending to horses, but, he said, 'I always found the dynamic between Creswell and those girls to be unpleasant . . . He would regularly run them down in front of people . . . I never witnessed any physical violence but regularly saw him shouting and being bad tempered towards them.' The group of girls he was referring to were Katie, Christina, Hayley and Rose.

By late February police were attempting to gather evidence about the alleged fall from Nelson and the supposed accident that Katie had had that had resulted in her bruising. As Creswell told it, she had been trampled by the horse as she put him into a field, getting tangled in his tackle and being dragged along the ground. Rose had claimed she'd seen her fall off a horse and hurt her jaw. At Jill Robinson's yard, as they tried to get to the bottom of the incident, the police heard another story, and as they made their enquiries a furious Creswell arrived, realising how close officers were getting to him. Still living with Christina in his mother's home in Greysteel in Derry, he had stayed close friends with Jill and saw her regularly. But while she backed up the story of an accident, she gave different details about how Katie had supposedly sustained the injuries – which the pathologist had said were from a sustained and brutal attack and sexual assault.

In early March, just weeks into the new investigation, Creswell was arrested and taken into custody. The PSNI released a simple statement:

A 33 year old man has been arrested by detectives investigating the death of a 21 year old woman at Altnagelvin Hospital on August 3rd, 2020 following an incident at an address in Gortnessy Meadows on August 3. He remains in custody at present. There are no further details.

At the station Creswell was confident. Just as he had been during his arrest for Abi Lyle almost a decade earlier, he was all talk, despite advice from his solicitor. This time he'd had more time to come up with a story, one that he believed was credible enough to explain some of his actions.

Asked why his DNA had been found in Katie Simpson's vaginal canal and on her pants and the jumper she was wearing, Creswell didn't flinch, telling police that he had been in a consensual sexual relationship with her for four years. He said that the day before her death, after the showjumping event, she had insisted they go to a place that she liked so they could have sex. However, he said, there were too many people there, so they drove to another area and had sex. He said they'd finished up and gone home and that he had spent the night in her bedroom with her, again having sex, while Christina slept in the next room with the two children. Crucially, he said that before he'd gone to bed with her younger sister, his partner Christina was up chatting with Rose.

He tried to stick to his story of having found Katie hanging, and to his claim that she had tried to take her own life before by driving into the central reservation of a road – the same story that Jill Robinson had told Paul Lusby. But police had confirmed that this accident happened because she'd fallen asleep at the wheel of her car. Creswell told officers that Katie was suffering from low self-esteem at the time of her death and that he had been worried about her in the run-up to it, even confiding his concerns to Robinson.

He insisted that Katie had been alive when he left to drop his children to his mother's home the following morning and that she had called one of them back to give them a hug. When he returned, he claimed, he found her hanging, her face to the wall, her lips almost 'kissing it'. He drew a rough sketch of how he had found her, but the length of the ligature had already been tested again and again and it was just not long enough. His version of events had not made sense and at one point he'd remarked about his own drawing: 'That doesn't make it long enough, does it?'

Creswell wasn't as confident when he was asked at length about Katie's phone. He initially claimed he'd no idea where it had been, but the GPS system on it showed that he had had it with him, including when he went to his mother's home. Eventually he claimed that he'd found Katie's phone and had hidden it in a field, but he couldn't give any explanation of why he'd done so. A search team made their way to Slaughtmanus Road in Killaloo, where he said he'd chucked the device, and found it. Later they would discover the messages that had been deleted, which were evidence of her liaison with Shane McCloskey and her fears around their relationship.

When quizzed about Katie and her relationships he admitted that he had lied when he said she had never had a boyfriend, saying that he and Katie had had an affair. Eventually he claimed that Katie had told him that Shane had stayed with her on the Saturday night but that they weren't in a sexual relationship. 'I never thought anything of it,' he said.

With regard to her injuries he said he could provide no explanation. He told police that at Robinson's yard, as they unloaded the horses after the show, she had told him that a horse had 'run over her ... or something like that' in the field but he only 'vaguely' remembered her saying something about her head. He didn't see any bruising on her body, he told officers. Asked about bringing Katie to the hospital he said that he 'dragged' her into the car and drove at speed. He said he'd hit a ramp on the way there and Katie had 'hit the roof' of the car.

When police confirmed that they hadn't found his own phone and asked him where it was he replied: "I've no idea". Asked what the password was should it be located he proceeded to tell them it was a sequence of numbers which spell out 'k-a-t-i-e'.

Officers were satisfied they had a strong enough case for the PPS, despite the opportunities missed by the previous inquiry – including the fact that Creswell's car had been returned with no forensic examination conducted. While no enquiries had been made at the time to establish the circumstances of Katie's supposed fall from the horse, and CCTV opportunities had been missed, the differing accounts and pathology findings meant that could be disproved.

Photographs had not been taken of Katie's injuries when she arrived at hospital, something that could have been requested by police, and no statements had been taken from medical staff until

February 2021, a month before Creswell's arrest. Still, police were confident that they had caught up with Creswell at last.

On the day of Creswell's arrest Hayley Robb provided the first of three statements to police. She gave an account of their phone calls. The first was as he was getting his children into the car to take them to his mother's. She told police that he told her that Katie was in the house. He rang her again, she said, on the way back from his mother's and talked about horse sales. All of a sudden, she said, she heard him screaming and he ordered her to ring an ambulance, which she did. She said that she made her way to Gortnessy and saw Creswell's car parked outside. She said the front door of the house was open. Her account was at odds with the CCTV footage gathered by the original investigation team, which showed both her and Creswell arriving at the house at the same time. She said she went into the house and saw blood on the stairwell and marked where it was on a plan of the house police had drawn up.

Rachel Lyle was attending court remotely on a Wednesday morning when her phone rang. Over the course of the pandemic she and other barristers had got used to appearing via site link in courtrooms across Northern Ireland, where Covid restrictions had created a whole new world of social distancing. She had her phone on silent but beside her at her desk should anything urgent come up. Her sister Abi was a prolific texter but only ever rang if there was something serious to say, so when she saw Abi's name pop up repeatedly on the phone she knew that something was wrong. She discreetly texted and said she'd be in touch as soon as she could and once she'd finished her hearing she grabbed the phone and hit the call button with a sense of anxiety in her stomach.

She'd phoned me and I was in court from home and I saw that it was something serious so I told her I would phone her back as soon as I could. When I did she was in hysterics and she told me that the police had just phoned. 'Johnny's killed somebody' she said. And she was so upset and she was blaming herself. She said to me 'I thought I'd done enough but I didn't and he's done something really bad, he's killed someone.' She felt so guilty and was crying over and again, saying 'that poor girl, that poor girl'. The police wanted to interview her while he was in custody so there was real time pressure on her and she had to literally dump everything; dump her day and go and be interviewed by the police that night and then the next day as well because he was in custody and they needed her interview to be able to charge him with Katie's murder. They needed her because of the strangling. Okay, so they had lifted him like, on maybe a Monday, and then they phoned her instead of having her interview ready and done before the arrest as you normally would. They arrested him and so it was like a retrospective. They did an initial interview with her on maybe Wednesday evening and then she had to go back on Thursday morning about the strangling. The police needed to prove that he had a history of strangling.

Unknown to Abi, the police had also contacted Sarah, the woman Creswell had exposed himself to in 2015. Like Abi, she was totally stunned by the news that he was in custody being interviewed about a murder and she couldn't believe that her own case had been dropped years before when, she believed, police hadn't trusted her story. Like Abi, she dropped everything and went to do what she could to help the investigation into Katie's death.

Days after his arrest, on Saturday 6 March, Creswell appeared via VideoLink at a special sitting of Dungannon Magistrates' Court. Had she lived, that day would have been Katie's twenty-second birthday. During the hearing a detective told the court he believed he could connect Creswell to a charge of murder. Details of Creswell's apparent mercy mission to Altnagelvin Hospital and the concerns of the medical staff on her arrival were relayed to the court, including the fact that there were no obvious ligature marks but there were unaccounted-for injuries on her body. The detective also told the court that Katie had hidden a new relationship from Creswell. 'It is our belief the defendant discovered this relationship. The day before the incident Katie had been showjumping in Lurgan. She was not permitted to drive her own car back home afterwards and was instructed to travel with the defendant, who ordered another person to drive her car.'

Creswell, the court heard, had controlled Katie and instilled fear in her, as evidenced by the messages on her phone. 'The messages recovered clearly indicate Katie was in immense fear of this man. He was constantly checking her phone and insisting on knowing the unlocking codes,' said Detective Sergeant James Brannigan, adding that Creswell 'controlled Katie since she was nine or ten and controls other females'. A defence barrister requested bail to be granted, pointing out that Creswell had answered all questions put to him. He said Creswell's family and friends had come together and offered a collective cash surety, and his partner, Christina, could surrender his passport. However,

District Judge Steven Keown threw out the application, ruling that the risks were too great to allow the accused to be released.

As Tanya Fowles closed her laptop she was incensed. While it was great that Creswell was finally facing charges for Katie's death she simply couldn't understand why it had taken so long and she believed that the police should also be investigated for the way they had handled the case. Days later she wrote again to the press office:

Further to my previous enquiries of December 2020 in respect of what has now been established as the murder of Katie Simpson, concerns of which were directly raised by me to Derry and Strabane District Police while she was still alive in ICU, and others after she passed away, will a full investigation be launched into: How this matter was deemed suicide absent very specific evidence and against the concerns of many including medical staff? Why were calls and reports of concerns ignored and who (job title) instructed these should not be actioned, followed up or responded to? Why were CID not permitted to take over this investigation and who (job title) blocked this? Have any officers been suspended or reported to PSD [the Professional Standards Department] as a direct result of their handling [and] lack of action on this matter? Finally, from my own perspective were my concerns dismissed and ignored because of my profession, which I disclosed upfront?

Tanya knew she was agitating, but she also wanted answers. How could so many aspects of the original investigation have gone in favour of the man now accused of murder? Was this incompetence or was there something else at play?

The response came quickly and was to the point: 'As this is a live investigation it would be inappropriate to comment at this time.'

Undeterred, Tanya wrote back: 'I'm not asking about the current live murder investigation. I'm asking about the forerunner to getting it actually taken seriously. That forms no part of the murder investigation which was removed from the control of Derry and Strabane PSNI. I have direct personal knowledge of this matter and I was fobbed off numerous times before. It won't be happening again. I'm offering a final opportunity with the original deadline or I will publish the enquiry in full and the detailed information I hold.' But the police were doubling down.

On 18 March Tanya wrote again:

Can a comment please be provided as to why PONI rejected a complaint in respect of the inaction of Derry and Strabane PSNI around failures to appropriately address the concerns around reports of the suspicious death of Katie Simpson, aged 21, in Altnagelvin Hospital. This was originally deemed a suicide and incorrectly investigated. The relevant individual who was reported to police by several persons has since been charged with murder – over 7 months after concerns were first raised. We have met with a number of sources who are extremely aggrieved by both police action and failure of PONI to appropriately assess their complaints. A point of very high relevance was the instruction given not to act on reported concerns and a failure to escalate enquiries beyond uniform. This is an extremely serious case against a domestic violence background, which is adding further to concerns on many levels as to how it was permitted. As well as comment around this, will an internal investigation be launched into the handling of the matter by PONI. Acknowledgement is requested and response by 4pm on Friday March 19th would be appreciated.

The response did come, but in the form of a document from the Department of Justice entitled *Police Misconduct, Performance and Attendance and Complaints Procedures*. Tanya was pointed to the section entitled 'Definition of a Complaint', which set out when the concerns of members of the public should be taken on board:

Complaints alleging misconduct can be received from members of the public who have had occasion to be well informed as to the facts of the incident. There is no need to record and process complaints from persons not involved in the incident. Thus someone views an incident on the TV or social media. They are not personally involved. Complaints should though be recorded if the member of the public was either personally involved in the incident or is a relative or friend of someone who was and who is acting on their behalf.

This placed Tanya's situation right into the terms of reference. However, the response continued: 'The rationale for our decision, therefore, was that at the time of the complaint, the complainant was not acting on behalf of Katie's family. I understand our rationale was communicated at the time, including the need for consent.'

Tanya couldn't believe what she was reading. Had the PSNI and now the Police Ombudsman of Northern Ireland suggested that it was only a member of someone's family who could complain or give information about a criminal offence? A day later, on Friday 19 March, she wrote:

It is unacceptable for a witness wanting to provide specific evidence to be rejected by the PSNI and then thereafter failed by PONI due to criteria. It is simply outrageous that more attention was not given to very specific concerns around the death of a 21 year old in a domestic violence situation. PONI governance, as it stands, amounts to a perpetrator's charter and fails to hold PSNI to account. This matter has been raised with the Minister for Justice and a comment is awaited. Initially we intended to ask if PONI would instigate an urgent investigation into the PSNI overall handling – or probably better to say mishandling of the Katie Simpson case, but our sources have no confidence in PONI. It is therefore intended to call for an independent inquiry into Derry and Strabane PSNI and the subsequent approach of PONI.

That same day this letter was sent to the Department of Justice:

Good afternoon,

In the course of covering a particular murder case which was originally deemed a suicide it emerged a member of the public, aware of issues, attempted to report matters of concern to police. These were ignored and while that position later changed the reporting person made a complaint to PONI as to the failure of the PSNI to act on concerns.

While not specifically referring to this case it transpires PONI's governance arrangements do not permit the investigation of the complaint against PSNI inaction if the reporting person is not a relative of or acting on behalf of a relative of the victim.

This is a striking flaw and one which could potentially jeopardise justice. It is also particularly concerning in a domestic violence environment where relatives may have been unaware of concerns and indeed it could suit perpetrators' agendas to effectively shut down investigation which they would be unlikely to generate. Can the minister please provide a comment in respect of the same and if she is willing to review the position. It has caused huge concern particularly among domestic violence awareness advocates.

As Tanya pressed for answers, police were continuing to gather any evidence that would be useful in the case against Creswell. While they were satisfied that they had strong circumstantial evidence, the motive for the murder of Katie was still unclear, as were some of the events that surrounded her arrival in hospital.

On 17 March 2021 Hayley Robb was brought back for another interview. This time she started to open up, admitting that she and Creswell were not just friends; they had been in a sexual relationship for almost 10 years, while he had also been with Christina Simpson, with whom he had two children. She began to paint a picture of the type of character Creswell was, saying that he was very controlling towards her and would often take her phone to monitor who she was talking with. He was particularly aggressive with her when she was in contact with or seeing other men. On one occasion, when she refused to have sex with him, Creswell lost his temper. He pushed her head against the window of a car and slapped her in the face, calling her a 'cunt' and a 'whore'. She told police that when she didn't report in on a night out he would contact her via Snapchat, something he had done with Katie the morning after her night with Shane. While Robb was clearly beginning to open up she went no further with her revelations to police, who recognised that she was one of many people scared of Creswell. They had no idea that she was still hiding Creswell's secrets.

Two months later Robb was back at the police station giving another interview. She told police she'd witnessed Creswell being violent to Christina and had seen him pull her by the hair across the ground before attacking her. She said she remembered Christina mouthing 'help' to her as he drove her away in their car. The most violence she herself had suffered had been some years before, when she was younger, and she said he'd mellowed to her in the previous few years. Christina, too, had told them that her arm had been broken during their relationship and that she was getting support from Women's Aid.

From prison Creswell continued to speak with Jill and Christina, but his absence meant that the carefully balanced relationships between the women had come under pressure. Desperate to salvage what she could of their business as Creswell languished in prison, Christina had tried to shore up their assets, but a row had broken out with Hayley Robb over money she said she was owed. Robb had not only allowed herself to be used by Creswell, she had also been guarantor for a £15,000 loan and had taken out two further loans for him of £6,500 and £10,000. Horse boxes and equipment were earmarked for her in a bid to pay back the money, but eventually the tension between the women reached breaking point and Robb decided that she was ready to come clean to police. On 25 June 2021, she went voluntarily to the officers investigating Katie's murder and told them that she wanted to tell the full story.

In an interview room, over the course of many hours, Robb said that on the Sunday before Katie was killed Creswell had arranged to meet with her the following day to prepare horses for sale and to have sex. As officers knew, she left Banbridge and got the first call from Creswell as he bundled the children into the car. He called her again after dropping them off, but this time she told police that he said Katie was at home, having taken the day off. While it took some time, she eventually admitted that Creswell had told her during the call that he had hit Katie the night before after finding out she'd been with Shane McCloskey. Robb told the cops that he admitted 'he gave her a hiding'. While Robb insisted she knew nothing of Creswell and Katie's sexual relationship she did drop a bombshell as she continued to reveal the events of that morning. Robb revealed that when Creswell arrived at the house in Gortnessy, instead of just grabbing the keys, as he had told officers, he had taken a cold shower and changed his clothes.

Robb said she 'never thought anything more of it' and told officers she believed this was a 'normal' thing to do. But she also revealed that he had ordered her to put his clothes in a bag and wash them, telling her to 'not breathe a word about it' – which the prosecution would use in its case – and he later said she was to tell anyone who asked that the bag contained horse clippers. She told officers that she saw a black strap on the banister and that on the way to the hospital he said he'd had difficulty removing Katie from it.

Robb said she went to the hospital with Creswell, with the bag of clothes in the back of her car, and later she went with Jill and him to the Foyle Bridge, where Christina joined them. As they sat in the car, she said, Creswell claimed he couldn't believe that Katie had hung herself and said he was suicidal himself. She later said she went to Jill Robinson's house and told her about the clothes and that Creswell wanted them washed. She also said she told her about his admission that he had hit Katie. She said she and Jill then travelled to an area called Fintona, where there was an outdoor public laundry facility and that she stayed in the car while Jill put the clothes in the machine.

Robb said she took time off after the events and that during that time Creswell had phoned her and asked her to clean up blood at the house as he didn't want Christina finding it. She stuck to that story until she was told that video footage taken by a scene of crime team that was shot immediately after she and Creswell left the house showed no blood. Pressed on this inconsistency, she said that Creswell had told her to clean it up that morning before they went to the hospital. 'He dragged me into this. I thought it was all innocent,' she said. When asked why she hadn't been forthright from the beginning about cleaning the blood and washing the clothes, Robb said that Creswell had control over her, had assaulted her and was in a sexual relationship with her. She said she had helped him out financially and detailed the loans she had taken out for him and the money she had given him. She said that Jill Robinson had told her to tell nobody about washing the clothes and explained to her how Katie had been trampled by a horse.

At the end of her lengthy interviews Robb was exhausted. She concluded that she had been controlled by Creswell since she was 18 and said she was frightened of what he would do to her if he discovered she had co-operated with the investigation.

Robb's statement was jaw-dropping. Not only did she describe an elaborate and organised cover-up, which she had been part of, her evidence also exposed a far more incompetent original investigation than had ever been imagined. The information was staggering and officers had no idea that such a large cover-up had been under way in the background. The fact that Creswell had changed his clothes could easily be checked on the body cams that police wore when they first interviewed him at the hospital. Sure enough, when they looked at the footage they could clearly see that Creswell was wearing a fresh top. Later it would emerge that an officer had indeed noticed it, but the detail had been buried in the police log of events and had not been followed up. CCTV of a woman leaving Gortnessy with a bag had also been noted but never followed up with the footage which had been collected at the house.

In the car on the bridge Creswell had been upset and crying. He'd asked Robb and Robinson, 'Do you think it was because of me?' They consoled him and told him that he wouldn't have hurt her and that he doted on her like nobody else. And the cover-up had begun.

Thanks to Hayley Robb officers finally had a picture of the bizarre cult-like structure that Creswell had formed around him and where each woman stood in the pecking order. They concluded that Jill Robinson, the eldest of the women, was like the boss, with a controlling influence over the others. She would later be identified from phone evidence as coaching the others what to say. In particular, officers believed, she had championed the narrative that Katie had been trampled by a horse and had instructed Hayley to ring the police after one of her statements were recorded to make sure that detail was included. Police also discovered that she had deleted many messages between herself and Rose. Police also believed she was using Rose as a conduit for Creswell to communicate with Christina from prison, and she had instructed Christina not to mention any domestic violence. Officers concluded that Jill was not in fear or under any duress.

But they had another issue as a result of Hayley Robb's admissions. They strengthened the case against Creswell, but the police were now dealing with a second layer of crimes against Katie Simpson. According to Robb, the women she believed were her friends had conspired with Creswell, as she lay dying, to cover up details of her death that should have led to a much earlier investigation into a possible murder. The women would all have to be brought in again and in all likelihood they too could face criminal charges.

CHAPTER 11

SEEKING BAIL

Justice O'Hara was confused for many reasons. 'Am I correct in saying the red flag was raised in the death of Miss Simpson by a doctor in Altnagelvin? Is that right?' Robin Steer, for the Crown, said yes, the judge was right. 'And what is understood to be, or what is alleged to be the cause of Miss Simpson's death. Is it strangulation or what?' the judge asked. Steer drew a breath before replying: 'The pathologist described it as being possible hanging. That's mainly on the face of information given to him by the Applicant [Creswell]. That is a result of his findings to date. But then we have the medical evidence from the doctor at the hospital saying the injuries to the neck are not consistent with a hanging.'

On video link to the court was Creswell, now desperate for bail after more than two months in custody. And playing out in his bail hearing was, for the first time, the case the Crown had against him and, indeed, its weaknesses. 'Essentially it's a circum-stantial case with regards to the actual death. The prosecution says she has died, but we simply say his account as hanging isn't credible,' Steer told the judge, explaining that Creswell's case was that he found Katie hanging and did what he did to save her, and that didn't tally with the injuries the doctors discovered on her body.

'But if that's right,' continued the Judge, 'and the pathologist should not – with all due respect to the pathologist – should not be signing off the cause of death on the basis of what somebody has told him. The pathologist should only be signing off the cause of death on the basis of a medical examination, and then says either "I can't say what the cause of death was' or 'The cause of death was consistent with A, B or C."'

'Yes,' replied Steer. 'All the pathologist can really say is possible hanging. He can't be any more conclusive than that and the prosecution can't say – and I accept – as per My Lord's question, we have evidence there was manual strangulation, rather than hanging or something of that type. It's simply unclear in terms of the medical evidence.' The judge looked shocked and said that while he wasn't intending to try the case that day, the prosecution was going to have an issue unless it advanced its position at a murder trial by focusing on a cause of death. Steer agreed that would be an issue as the medical injuries were not conclusive either. However, he said, that wouldn't preclude a murder trial on the basis of other evidence in the case. 'It's simply that the medical evidence is inconclusive.'

Justice O'Hara started to summarise the case, at one point getting confused about the relationship between Creswell and the Simpson girls and asking if he had two children with Christina and another by a second sister. 'But Christina Simpson has children by Mr Creswell, is that right? . . . And the prosecution case is that Mr Creswell was also having a sexual relationship with Katie Simpson?'

'And,' interrupted Steer, 'he was also having a relationship with another female referred to as "H" from 2009 to 2019.'

The judge pointed to the relationship with Abi Lyle and Creswell's conviction for assaults on her and asked the prosecution what the relevance of the relationship with H was. 'She has come forward to police since the death to say she was in a long-term relationship with him and that he had also been assaulting her. She's provided an ABE [achieving best evidence] interview,' Steer said.

Money borrowed by Creswell was detailed to the judge, including a £10,000 loan from H, who had also acted as guarantor for another £15,000 of borrowings; a Credit Union loan taken out by Katie Simpson to the tune of £10,000; and his requests for a loan from Katie's mother as her daughter lay dying in the intensive care unit.

'And Christina Simpson has now come forward and said she was regularly and frequently assaulted by Mr Creswell?' the judge asked, to which Steer replied: 'Yes, she has provided an ABE to say she was frequently assaulted by him, that he broke her arm in 2018 and police have advised me just this morning that a childminder has come forward in the last 48 hours, explaining her concerns about Christina, that she was appearing with bruising when she was looking after the children, and in particular the broken arm in 2018. The childminder didn't believe her account of how her arm came to be broken and the childminder passed those concerns on to Social Services back in 2018, before this happened.'

'Is it likely, Mr Steer, that as a result of these further statements being made by a range of people, that Mr Creswell is going to face many more, many more charges than the murder charge?' the judge asked. Steer replied that he didn't know but that the police were taking a view that there were more and more people coming forward all the time. Just 24 hours before the bail hearing a well-respected horse trainer had been speaking to police about what he knew about his treatment of Christina. 'So yes, I'm sure police will have to look at other charges,' said Steer.

'So, the concern here; you've got a concern here . . . what you have is not just a murder charge – as if a murder charge wasn't serious enough on its own – but you've got a long-term pattern of violent behaviour by Mr Creswell. There's concern about inter-ference with witnesses. There's a concern about whether there's a potential risk of further offences, and you are also asserting there is a risk of absconding over the border where he went on a previous occasion when he was charged? And he doesn't actually have any financial ties to Northern Ireland?' asked Justice O'Hara.

While Creswell would have been right to think that his house of cards was beginning to fall, with both Hayley Robb and Christina clearly breaking their omertà with the prosecution case against him, the same couldn't be said for the loyal Jill Robinson. She had put up a bail surety for him of £10,000 and the judge was told that while she was co-operating with police about a relationship she had been in with Creswell she was not alleging that she had been controlled or assaulted. 'There's an allegation from one of the other females, Abigail Lyle, who is the female of whom he is convicted of the assaults on; the applicant had told Abigail Lyle he also assaulted Jill Robinson,' Steer said.

'Okay. Is the issue in relation to sureties . . . the bail motion says there's four cash sureties. £10,000 has been lodged into the client account of the defendant's solicitor's firm and more money is available. Of course, he should have more money available because he's been borrowing significantly from young women over the years. Your proposition is bail should be refused and if bail is granted it should be off substantial surety.'

'Yes, primarily it's the risk of further offences, risk of further offending against females as evidenced by the document and also risk of interference with witnesses,' Steer said.

Kevin Mallon, defence counsel, was next to be heard. He told the judge that it was his client's position that the hearing was an attempt by the prosecution to raise a lot of bad character evidence against him.

Now there clearly will, My Lord, in relation to the various individuals identified, be it Chloe Scott, Abigail Lyle, H, E – there are a number of anonymised individuals – there are very, very significant issues with regards to the admissibility of that evidence. And really when one seeks to critically assess the written submission there is no direct evidence of involvement of any murder by Mr Creswell. There is what the prosecution appears to be suggesting to the court, a circumstantial case, where even on its own admission, there are very, very significant issues surrounding causation. If one goes to paragraph 12 of the written submission, in terms of the specific and direct question Your Lordship asked, a post-mortem performed on 11 August 2020 recorded possible hanging.

It seemed that Creswell was intent on using police incompetence to his advantage at trial. 'From the day of the incident on 3 August until the post-mortem on 11 August, a period of some eight days, there must assuredly have been communication with investigating police and the forensic pathologist, who was to conduct the post-mortem. It's perhaps somewhat trite to suggest Mr Bentley made his findings and conducted a post-mortem, and in his conclusions or summary, from what he was told by the accused. That simply wouldn't happen and it's nonsense to suggest that would happen.'

The judge agreed: 'It certainly shouldn't happen.'

Mallon went on:

As Your Lordship knows post-mortem examinations are very invasive and certainly here in relation to the brain and indeed in relation to any injury to the neck the pathologist from a forensic pathologist perspective would focus on those issues, and he has concluded there remains the possibility of hanging here. The prosecution recognised and clearly recognised there is a difficulty for them in this case, based primarily on an inability to, as it were, lay to rest the issue of causation. If one pauses for a moment to consider the matters that are raised in relation to Dr Campbell, who in my understanding is an accident and emergency consultant in trauma. Dr Campbell – now I haven't seen his formal statement of evidence – but that portion of the prosecution submission . . . makes a number of assumptions that are clearly beyond his sphere of competence. Clearly, My Lord, that evidence itself and what he asserts will be subject to very strong challenge.

The judge agreed to see Dr Campbell's statement and other medical evidence from the prosecution before he decided on bail.

Mallon said he would like to see it too: 'If Your Lordship looks at what Dr Campbell said. He says he'd never encountered a situation where someone had put someone into a car who was unconscious and not breathing. The accused was taking the deceased to hospital. He then speaks about some vagueness on the part . . .'

The judge interrupted: 'Sorry, sorry. Is it right she was then resuscitated by paramedics?'

'Again, I haven't seen any paramedics' report, My Lord. I haven't seen any. I don't have the deposition, or I should say more appropriately, the papers. But it's quite clear that Dr Campbell is trespassing . . .' Mallon said.

Justice O'Hara said he needed to see more evidence from the prosecution about its murder charge to see how strong the case was.

That's an issue to which I'm entitled to enquire if it's a strong case that it's a murder. Let's take the scenario that there's a strong case to believe a murder has been committed here and he's also got a record from some years ago for violent attacks on a former partner, and who has been raising loans, including from the dead girl, and has been having a sexual relationship with her. And other people are now coming forward. There may be issues, in fact there would be issues about the strength of the case, about interference with witnesses and potentially about further offences. There might also be an issue about flight, because not just on an academic basis, but there was an issue about him leaving the jurisdiction in 2015 for a significantly less serious allegation of indecent exposure.

The flight risk related to the unresolved case of Sarah, which the PSNI had closed because they couldn't, despite their best efforts, locate Creswell, who was at that point living with his father, Herbie Lusby, in Donegal and travelling quite openly into the North. Mallon told the court exactly that.

I can deal with that very briefly if Your Lordship would just permit me. He did go . . . he moved across the border to live with his father. But he was working on a daily basis at a yard in Antrim . . . And police didn't seek to arrest him. I know, My Lord, it's been a long time since I was in the bail courts. It's the first time I've had to deal with what I would say is as lengthy a prosecution submission, because they appear in this case to be throwing everything including the kitchen sink at this. They are inserting matters . . . One has a situation, My Lord, and I just make this point; there's an assertion, an assertion that in relation to a single mobile phone message comprising some 15 words, that the prosecution are saying the police think it was the accused that sent it. I know there is a Professor Malcolm Coulthard, a professor of linguistics that deals with idiosyncratic texting and idiosyncratic messaging and fifteen words would not allow him to come to any conclusion that would not just weakly support, simply couldn't support what the prosecution are asserting . . . My Lord, with the greatest respect, if you take as a starting point, and I won't press this, My Lord, because I can perceive where Your Lordship is going with regards to clearly adjourning this application to get additional information. But if the starting point in any murder

case is that of causation and causation to which an individual accused of that murder can be connected, then the
prosecution case is significantly wanting, because what it is
seeking to do . . . is to rely on bad character. And to say
two witnesses came forward last night; I don't know what
the dynamic of this investigation is, but it's bad character
evidence from anonymised sources, some of whom have
waited nine months to contact police. You've a situation
in relation to the primary concern because it's focused on
the bad character. This conviction was recorded against my
client in Dungannon Crown Court in 2010, for offences that
are alleged to have occurred between February and August
2009. He received a six-month sentence. A six-month
sentence in relation to a number of incidents of domestic
violence and there is a world of difference, they are absolutely seas apart. An incident of domestic violence in 2009
and an alleged murder in August 2020. This case is absent
any evidence or any direct evidence to connect my client the
accused to this offence. There's material which will be challenged in terms of admissibility, to say he was perhaps, if one
wants to use a fairly colourful phrase, a philanderer. But you
can be a philanderer and not be a murderer.

Justice O'Hara intervened: 'He's worse than that, Mr Mallon.
He's not just a philanderer. He's a violent philanderer in that he
attacked a previous partner. He's also a philanderer who raises
money from . . . . In the prosecution case, he has loans from the
dead sister of his current partner. A twenty-one-year-old girl. He
gets a loan from her and he gets her to guarantee a further loan.'

Mallon insisted that he hadn't sat in on the interview but that his instruction was that a lot of the bad character evidence had never been put to Creswell during the interview. But the judge was cautious. While he assumed that there had been an extensive police investigation over six or seven months, he had no idea how lax the original probe had been. But he was intent on focusing on the medical evidence when it came to his decision about bail.

I presume he was interviewed initially and then perhaps interviewed again. We'll have to get into that at some point. Mr Mallon, I'm going to allow the prosecution some latitude. Mr Steer, I'm not satisfied . . . at the moment I want to see the pathologist report and I want to see whatever statement Dr Campbell has made and whatever medical records there are in relation to Dr Campbell's . . . from Altnagelvin I presume? . . . . I want to see whatever medical records are available from Altnagelvin, Dr Campbell's statement and Mr Bentley's statement.

Steer told the court that police had gone to Dr Campbell but that there had been a delay – between August and December police hadn't been investigating the case. 'Then DC Brannigan became involved, I think from about December, and the investigation really commenced then,' Steer admitted. 'And then a lot of allegations have been coming in more recently after the interview. I'll perhaps set that out better with a better timeline in relation to those steps as well.'

The judge then looked to the video link with DS Brannigan. 'When was the most recent interview with Mr Creswell, Detective Sergeant?'

Brannigan replied that the first time he was interviewed was under caution on 2 March and that he was charged on 6 March.

'Okay. And is there a statement from Dr Campbell from Altnagelvin?'

'There is one statement from Dr Campbell. We've taken statements from a number of doctors and nurses. We only provided one sample statement because they pretty much say the same thing, but we are happy to provide all the statements if needed from all the doctors and nurses.'

Justice O'Hara said, 'Thank you very much. Let's get the medical statements, Dr Campbell's statement, the medical records and the pathologist's report. There's a question mark at the start of this case which is relevant to the bail application on whether in fact the charge of murder . . . how well-founded that is. Mr Creswell can't be denied bail on the basis he's not a very nice guy. He's denied bail if there's risk of further offending, interference with witnesses or absconding, to give you the summary of what the main grounds are.'

As the investigations continued, with the case taking a stronger turn thanks to Hayley Robb's statements, Justice O'Hara returned his verdict and granted bail. Creswell was under strict orders, including being barred from living with any women. The judge cited the autopsy report in his decision. 'For now I have a case full of suspicion but, it seems to me, short on proof,' he said. The judge stressed that circumstances would change if any further charges were brought and, with total sureties of £60,000, ordered Creswell to live at an address in Larne, County Antrim and forbade him from entering Armagh. The judge also directed: 'No woman or girl is to live at that house while Mr Creswell is living there.'

Creswell was delighted, but his bail sureties soon fell through. But by June he had a new collection of money to offer the courts. Prosecutors again tried to make the case that he shouldn't be released, citing the cold shower, the washing of his clothes, cleaning blood off the bannisters and the meeting in the car on the Derry Bridge as Katie lay dying, and stressing that witnesses had come forward while Creswell was in custody. Mr Justice O'Hara noted the new evidence but said he was satisfied bail could be granted at £30,000 with strict conditions, including banning Creswell from attending any equestrian events, selling horse stock, entering County Armagh and having contact with any witnesses.

Keeping him away from witnesses was vital. The police investigation had moved forward, thanks to Robb, but they believed Creswell's hold was still strong, even from prison, and it was taking a long time to unravel the accounts. In particular, Rose was proving problematic. She had never gone back to live with Creswell and Christina after Katie's death, but she had kept in touch, first moving in with Jill Robinson and later moving to the UK, where she would be first arrested in August, a year after the murder. She had made a number of statements in the aftermath that police believed were false. The first was in October 2022, when she said that Katie had been trampled by a horse, a claim that officers were confident had been totally discredited. She had also told officers that she had chatted to Katie on the Sunday night when she returned home with Creswell before her death. That even went against Creswell's account that he had followed her into the house and she had made her way upstairs without talking to anyone. Common sense also told officers that someone who had taken a beating, as Katie had, was unlikely to be in the mood to chat. Rose had insisted she wasn't afraid of Creswell and said he had no hold over her. She had stuck with her story that she had brought him a cup of tea and that while she was in work Katie had hung herself.

Within months the charges against Creswell included one of rape. Robb, Robinson and De Montmorency Wright, all of whom were yet to be named, had been charged with helping him in the cover-up and had entered not guilty pleas. The court was told that a huge volume of mobile phone evidence was still being collated by an analyst, but the delay to move on to the Crown Court for trial was making headlines. As the case against Creswell repeatedly came up for mention with no progress a judge warned the Public Prosecution Service (PPS) that they needed to hurry things along. District Judge Barney McElhom noted that Creswell had first appeared in court in March 2021, 'which is 18 months plus'. His defence team added: 'The date of the alleged offence was long before that.' Judge McElhom continued, 'I don't know what the issues are, whether that's evidential problems or whatever. But between the directing officer, PPS and external counsel I want progress by the next date. It is a murder case. We don't get more serious than that. I repeat, I don't know what the issues are, but it might reach the point where I issue a warning and I set a committal date. They either meet it or they don't.' But the delays would continue as the PPS considered what case it might take against the women who had been identified as helping Creswell cover up his alleged crimes.

Still the wheels of justice creaked along and there was a further delay to a committal hearing scheduled for February 2023. In March 2023 the identities of three women were revealed, along with the charges they faced. Documents entered at Derry Magistrates' Court showed that Rose De Montmorency Wright, then 22, was accused of withholding information between 9 October 2020 and 13 October 2021, knowing Creswell had committed assault. Hayley Robb, then 29, faced four counts of withholding information between 2 August 2020 and 26 June 2021. Jill Robinson, then 41, was accused, with the others, of perverting the course of justice by taking Creswell's clothes on 3 August 2020 and washing them in an outdoor launderette. Within a month, they all stood accused of charges linked to the murder of Katie.

Rose returned to appear in person in Northern Ireland but went back to the UK, where she continued to event, and was even praised after finishing tenth at the Blair Castle International Horse Trials in Scotland in September. The following day she congratulated herself for being one of only two riders to complete the course. 'Matilda was a complete legend storming around a tough 3*L to finish sixth. We were one of two people clear inside the time and she jumped a super round today. Proud of her is an understatement! A massive thank you to everyone who has helped get us here.'

While Rose held strong, continuing with her life, Hayley Robb was suffering hugely with what had gone on and the realisation that she had been used and abused by Creswell, who she now believed had murdered Katie. In December 2023 she switched her plea and admitted her role in the cover-up, which changed the course of the case for everyone. Lawyers for Robb had asked for the charges to be put to her again at a review hearing of the case at Laganside Crown Court, at which point she broke down in tears and admitted all charges. Remaining on bail, she was told she'd be sentenced at the conclusion of the overall trial. But, most important for the police, she was still willing to give evidence against Creswell. Ironically, the woman he had controlled since she was just 18 years of age was going to become a star witness in his murder trial.

CHAPTER 12

THE TRIAL

It had been a long day in court and one of the most detailed openings many seasoned reporters had ever heard. It was 21 April 2024 and Creswell, described as a horse trainer, stood accused of the rape and murder of the young showjumper Katie Simpson, in what the court was told was a jealous rage. At Coleraine Crown Court, Creswell stood in the dock and listened intently as prosecution counsel Sam Magee KC set out the circumstances of the case.

It is the prosecution case that the defendant raped Katie. He murdered her. He made efforts to cover up her death by trying to make it look like a suicide. In the hours leading up to [her] death, he was with Katie. He was the last person to see her alive. At that time, he was the only person with Katie, or certainly the only adult. The prosecution say that it was a calculating and deceitful episode. Having strangled her, he created a fiction, pretending to others that he had found Katie hanging in a stairwell from a strap, pretending to medical staff that she had taken her own life. But the prosecution say that in an act of violent and desirous rage he had taken her life at the age of only just twenty-one. He then lied and lied and lied to mislead those trying to get to the bottom of what happened.

In the dock Creswell looked around, apparently feeling quite confident, despite the predicament he found himself in, and certain that he could fight the case, against the best advice of his legal team. Addressing the jury, Magee told them that it would be their task to determine the truth and to decide if Creswell had murdered and raped Katie Simpson or if there was reasonable doubt that he had. Magee explained the trial process and that they needed to approach the case with an open mind and face the trial in a 'solemn and dispassionate' way. 'Prejudice and sympathy should form no part of your reasoning,' he told the jury of eight men and four women. He then handed them the Bill of Indictment that set out the charges against Creswell. 'You will see that Mr Creswell faces two charges . . . the first count is murder and the second count is rape. Each count comes in two parts; the statement of offence and the particulars of offence.'

The jury listened intently as Magee patiently explained the elements of murder that must be proved before they would even consider convicting the accused.

First of all we must prove to you that Katie Simpson died, now there is not likely to be any dispute in relation to that. We must also prove when she died which is not likely to trouble you in this trial. Most importantly we must prove to you that it was Mr Creswell that caused her death and that when he did so he was intending to kill her or cause her really serious harm. Those issues are likely to be the matters most important in this case because Mr Creswell may say that he was just an innocent party in all this; a Good Samaritan who came across Katie Simpson's body having attempted to take her own life. He may say he did his best to seek medical attention and to save her. If, having heard all the evidence, you think that might be the case then it follows that the prosecution would not have proved beyond reasonable doubt. The prosecution says in this case that that version of events is untrue. If having heard all the evidence you are sure that Mr Creswell was the individual who assaulted her and did so in a manner for her to be fatally injured or to cause her serious harm before he set about covering it up, then you must find him guilty of murder. Only if you are sure.

Magee then moved to the second offence of rape. 'The prosecution case is that some point prior to the killing or in the course of the assault which led to her death that Jonathan Creswell raped her. You will hear how there had been a sexual relationship between the two but at the time he killed her Katie Simpson was in the early stages of a relationship with another man.' The prosecution, he said, would argue that if the pair were proved to have had sex before her death it wouldn't have been consensual on Katie's part. 'Coercion is not consent. Overbearing a person's will is not consent.'

Magee finally turned to the evidence the jury was about to hear, with what he said was a 'health warning'.

The first thing I want to tell you about is the evidence you will hear about the person who is the victim in this case,

Katie Simpson. Katie was just 21 years old when she died. Katie, like the defendant and many other witnesses in the case, was heavily involved in the equestrian scene here in Northern Ireland. One will tell you she was a fun outgoing girl. Others will say she was cheerful in the days leading up to her death. One friend will tell you how she was the sort of person to work through her problems. Katie had a number of siblings, one of whom was her sister Christina or Nina. Nina Simpson was at that time the long-term partner of Jonathan Creswell. They had two children; a girl aged three and a boy of six months. Katie had been living with them for a few months . . . Katie had taken a keen interest in horses from an early age. It was there the two sisters became acquainted with the defendant . . . After a time the defendant and Nina became an item. Over recent times they worked together in horses themselves and had about twenty horses. Katie worked for the defendant looking after training and running the horses. She would ride for various individuals at events including a lady called Jill Robinson who she was riding for the day before she was found.

Magee went on to say that Matthew Lusby would give evidence of how Creswell was difficult with the women around him and how Katie was under his 'spell'. (Lusby's father was Paul, one of the first whistleblowers who had tried to alert police, but he wasn't in court to witness this final takedown of Creswell.) 'Lusby will tell you that Katie was on the worst end of Creswell's behaviour. Although his behaviour was controlling, he felt, he was not physically violent to his knowledge. He will say she seemed fearful, and happy when he wasn't around.' Other friends, Magee said, were concerned about her too and her interactions with Creswell, who would shout at her. 'The defendant and Katie were also involved in a sexual relationship. The prosecution will say that not only was Katie fearful but that she had every reason to be, given her ultimate fate.' The description of what there was between Katie and Creswell as a 'sexual relationship' made it sound consensual, but as Magee's opening remarks continued it became clear that she had been groomed by him since she was a child and that she was terrified of him.

Details of Katie's new relationship with Shane McCloskey were described to the jury, along with how frightened she was that Creswell would discover it. Witnesses would describe to the court how Katie seemed 'under his spell' the more time she spent with him and Christina, said Magee. 'But he would shout and be bad-tempered with her. She seemed fearful of him.'

The evidence would principally deal with the events of the weekend before she was taken to hospital and Katie's night out with friends, which was followed by Shane McCloskey's arrival at her mum's house. The scenario came alive in the courtroom, the jury listening intently and Creswell sitting in the dock, his head bowed. 'Katie called to her mum's house and made arrangements to stay. Her mum, Noeleen Simpson, will give evidence how she saw Katie that afternoon and that she was in good form and appeared to be texting a lot. She asked Katie if she had a boyfriend but she said no. In her mum's mind, Katie seemed distant and nervous,' he said. Katie and her pal went to the pub in the Moy. Their conversation was about horses and people they knew and Katie admitted that she'd started going out with

Shane McCloskey. 'You will hear about a man called Paul Lusby. He had become aware of Katie's attraction to Shane but that she was anxious to keep it quiet that she was seeing him,' the jury were told.

As the night wore on Katie asked her friend if she minded if she left early as she wanted to meet Shane at her mother's house.

By the beginning of August they were in the very early stages of their relationship but in contact every day. Mr McCloskey also knew the defendant as they were both involved in the local equestrian scene. Mr McCloskey will tell you that Creswell knew he had an interest in Katie. He noticed from the time he started seeing Katie that Mr Creswell had stopped mentioning her to him. He also became aware that Katie wouldn't contact him when in Creswell's company. He told her he wanted to see her more often but she said she would have to ask the defendant about that, telling Mr McCloskey not to say anything to him himself. You will hear evidence that it appeared that Creswell was trying to blacken McCloskey to Katie Simpson and turn her against him, the reasons for which, say the prosecution, are very obvious.

Snapchat photographs that Katie had posted that evening showed her looking happy, and her friend Chloe Scott would tell the jury over the course of the trial that her friend 'looked glowing'. As midnight approached McCloskey arrived at Katie's mother's home and Katie was in her pyjamas but let him in, unknown to her mum and the others in the house. 'The two spent the night together having intercourse for the first time.'

Following a break the jury were told that mobile phone evidence would play a large part in the trial; telephone calls, mobile text messages and cell site analysis of the movements of individual phones. A schedule of evidence was presented to them and they were guided to pink, green and dark blue entries. 'Entries in pink refer to the phone of Katie, green is Creswell and dark blue is Shane McCloskey,' Magee explained.

He directed the jury to the schedule relating to the morning of Sunday 2 August between 5 and 7am, when Katie and Shane McCloskey were up and about after their night together. The document showed how Creswell started to call Katie at 5:49am, then phoned again at 5:56am, at which point he sent the chat message: 'You reply to my snap right now.' By 6:15am, when Katie was on the road to Omagh to pick up a horse, Creswell called her for approximately two minutes. 'Why was he so irate? What had he sent to her on Snapchat to demand a reply in such aggressive terms and what might this tell you of his attitude?' the jury was asked.

By 7am Katie and McCloskey had started a series of text message exchanges, which would continue throughout the day. At first they were shy and coy but as the day wore on Katie started to delete them.

The first one, sent from Shane to Katie, read: 'I really enjoyed last night. ♥ I just hope you don't regret anything. xxxxxx.'

Katie wrote back: 'I did and I don't. I don't want you thinking I'm a whore or anything. I don't usually do that. xxxxx'

Shane: 'No I know you are not a whore. Stop worrying. Sure we ain't seeing anyone else. I just want you. I swear. xxxxx'

Katie: 'Ok. Ok. I'm glad you came. Xxxxxx'

Shane: '♥ I am too. Xxxxx'

Later in the morning Katie texted again: 'Just walking Nelson out of the field and he looks fresh. You left a mark on my neck.'

Shane responded, 'Good luck with him. Oh fuck sorry. What you gonna say now LOL. xxxxxx'.

As the jury listened intently Magee told them that the messages had been deleted from Katie's phone by the time it was found but were still on McCloskey's.

'Katie deleted them or someone with possession of her phone deleted them. Ask yourselves why? The prosecution will say the reason is that Jonathan Creswell wouldn't be happy that Katie was sleeping with Shane. Either Katie deleted them or he did. The prosecution says Katie was trying to hide them from Creswell.'

The jury were then directed to look forward to messages sent between 7 and 8am that morning, when Katie was becoming concerned about the marks on her neck and that Creswell might find out she and Shane had been together.

At 7am she texted Shane: 'I put makeup over it. I hope nobody notices. Xxxxx'

Shane: 'You kept getting me to bite your neck. What will you do if Johnny sees it?'

Katie: 'I like it. I don't know. Hoping he doesn't.'

Shane: 'Yeah if he does you are fucked. Really glad you woke up last night. LOL xxxxx'

But by 7:45am Katie's mood wasn't so jovial. She texted Shane: 'I said to Johnny I haven't been talking to you since yesterday at the show. X' At that point, Magee told the jury, Shane had been seen driving on the road away from Katie's mum's house and informed Katie, to which she responded 'Oh shit.'

But Shane reassured her: 'I'll just say it wasn't me. I was going that hard it could have been anyone. It could be the talk of the show today . . . I keep thinking why did you ask last night would I get mad if you were meeting someone else? X'

In the background, Magee said, 'tongues had started to wag' and Creswell had heard that Shane had been spotted.

'Katie Simpson was in good form that morning. She was a bit tired but she jumped well and cleared two rounds. She had nothing to be sorry about and had even ordered herself new shoes. She had everything to live for and especially with her new relationship,' said Magee. 'But the telephone evidence indicates that, as the day wears on, both Katie and Shane are getting concerned. Messages deleted from her phone between the two of them demonstrate this. Messages which didn't refer to what had happened the night before weren't deleted and she had tried to get Shane to send a false narrative in a series of text messages.'

By 14:35, the court heard, Creswell had begun his own enquiries and Katie had texted Shane: 'Johnny asked me where you were and I said I haven't spoken to you since the show. He will probably ring you and ask you what you were doing this morning because . . .'

At 15:50 Creswell texted McCloskey: 'Shane. I'm in the toilet having a shit and someone is in the cubicle beside me . . . And I don't want them hearing.'

Shane responded: 'Nice. Enjoy the big push.' A four-minute phone call followed, during which Creswell quizzed Shane on where he'd been the night before. 'Shane will say he lied,' Magee told the jury. 'The defendant told him he'd been seen on the road and was questioning what the truth was. He was angry and suspicious that Shane and Katie had spent the night together and Katie was terrified of Creswell finding out.'

In the aftermath, the court heard, McCloskey tried to ring Katie, but Creswell was in control of her phone. The movement of phones, the jury heard, would prove that Katie and Creswell were together from five o'clock that night.

'The phones are together in her car,' said Magee. 'Evidence will tell you they left Lurgan and made their way to Robinson's yard. Katie is in the company of Creswell and she seems to have travelled in a horsebox. They arrive there around five p.m. The prosecution will say that from that time on they were together and first stayed in that general area until six-fifty p.m. During that time Shane is trying to get hold of Katie, to no avail. And the last significant outgoing activity is at seven p.m. from her phone to Rose De Montmorency Wright . . . after that there is no activity until eleven-forty p.m. that night.'

The GPS evidence, the jury heard, would show that the phones were moved at 7pm to Strabane, where they remained for two hours, during which time Creswell and Katie were alone. At 8:07pm Shane McCloskey rang again, and again at 8:20pm, but both calls went unanswered. Shane continued to ring – at 21:11pm, 21:15pm, 21:30pm and 22:13pm, at which point he sent a text: 'Have I done something wrong?'

'Why is she not getting back to him after all the loving messages?' asked Magee. 'What happened?'

At 22:16pm Shane texted: 'Is it after last night have you changed your mind or what?' The car, the jury heard, had moved from Strabane towards Lifford and by 11pm was coming back towards Claudy when Shane sent another text – 'a pivotal message'. 'I really wanted this to work. I didn't drive an hour and half to sleep with you if that is what you thought. Xxx'

Magee repeated the text and then stood back, considering the jury:

This was Jonathan Creswell's worst fear. What he didn't want. They'd had sex the night before. This was a pivotal moment. You see, the prosecution will say that Katie had carefully deleted messages between herself and Shane McCloskey to ensure that the defendant couldn't find proof of them having slept together the night before. She then made Shane send messages, fake messages, pretending he had been in his own bed in order to defeat the gossip of Shane being on the road near her home in the early morning. The prosecution will say the defendant was in actual control of her phone that night just like she had feared he would be. Hence the lack of contact . . . the lack of calls . . . the lack of texts, never mind the fact, as you will hear shortly, that Creswell had that phone in his possession the following morning as Katie lay dying . . . Once Jonathan Creswell saw that message, the prosecution says, Katie's fate was sealed . . . He was now in receipt of incontrovertible evidence that she had tried to cover it up.

While Shane was trying to contact Katie he also sent Creswell a message at 23:20pm: 'Is everything OK Sir?'

'It must have been those texts that prompted Johnny Creswell not to reply to Shane on his own phone but to reply on Katie's phone, which we say he had control of. At 23:29 you will see a message from Katie's phone to Shane McCloskey: 'FFS' – an abbreviation used by many as for fuck's sake – 'Just home long night what part of last night do you think made me change my mind????? ☺'

The prosecution would tell the court that Creswell sent the message, the first outgoing activity on Katie's phone in five hours. Creswell also sent a message to Shane from his own phone: 'Yes lad. Horse sold. Lie in for me in the morning.'

But Katie, in all the communications examined on her phone, had never used the abbreviation FFS. Creswell, on the other hand, had used it 241 times.

After midnight Katie's Facebook Messenger sent Shane McCloskey a note, a method of communication she had never used to contact him before. 'Are you sleeping? Just in now. Chat in the morning.'

Magee moved to the following morning at Gortnessy and the calls and movements that the jury would hear. Christina, the court heard, had awoken at 4.30am in the house in Derry to find Creswell sleeping in bed with her younger sister Katie. She went back to bed, the court heard, but then she left the house at 6am. Before she left she saw him sleeping in the spare room. At 6:40am Creswell phoned Rose, who was asleep downstairs on the couch. Rose, the court heard, would say that she left the house at 7:07am, taking Creswell's car, the one he'd travelled in the night before, which was unusual as she would usually take Katie's car, but she told police that it was unreliable. Shane McCloskey then sent two text messages to Katie. The first read: 'Good morning. Hope everything is OK.'

'It certainly wasn't okay,' said Magee. 'Shane McCloskey, having sent that message at 7:19am, then tried to call her but unsuccessfully. At the very same time Jonathan Creswell left the house with his children to take them to his mother's house in Greysteel, arriving there around eight o'clock. This time he was on the phone again to Rose De Montmorency Wright while Katie's phone was on the move with him. The prosecution says that he had taken her phone with him. You have to ask yourselves, why would he do that? The prosecution says that at that time Katie was in no state to use her phone. We say sometime before he left that house he had assaulted Katie, leaving her for dead.'

The jury were then shown the CCTV retrieved from the house showing the movements of cars to and from it and the various members of the household leaving for work.

But Creswell was about to start to squirm in the dock. The jury were told that they were going to hear the call between him and the ambulance services as he said he was on the way to Altnagelvin. For the prosecution this was one of the most important arguments to get right. They were anxious the jury did not come away thinking, as Creswell would claim, that he had done his best to save Katie's life.

You could hear a pin drop in the courtroom as Creswell's voice echoed out over the crackling phone line: 'Oh the poor wee girl, the poor wee girl,' he wailed at a call handler. Creswell was instructed to get Katie into the back seat or flat on the ground and in the courtroom his voice was heard breathlessly counting: 'Six. Seven . . .'

'Get her flat on her back and remove any pillows from beneath her head there,' the call operator instructs. Creswell shouts: 'Breathe . . . Breathe . . . I'm pumping, what do I do? One, two, three, four . . . one, two, three, four . . . one, two, three, four . . . one, two, three, four . . . Do I breathe into her mouth? . . . One, two, three, four.' The operator counts with Creswell as they wait for the ambulance to arrive. 'Oh my God . . . one, two, three, four . . . I think I'm hurting her . . . one, two, three, four . . . There is nothing happening here . . . one, two, three, four . . . They can see me . . . one, two, three, four . . . one, two, three, four . . . He's coming.' The operator encourages Creswell for the last few seconds and assures him: 'They are going to take over.'

In the dock Creswell's shoulders seemed to sag as Magee looked to the jury. 'It will be suggested that Mr Creswell made the best efforts to save the life of Katie Simpson. He sounds stressed, concerned, anxious, making his best efforts and focused on Katie's welfare, doesn't he? Members of the jury, you might think he was someone who was singularly focused on saving the life of a loved one.'

However, Magee said, Creswell was only pretending to save her life and three minutes into that call the ambulance services phone evidence would show that he was in fact focused on Katie's mobile, which he activated, unlocked, placed into airplane mode and then locked again. 'Why is he doing that?' He again played the recording for the jury at the exact point that happened, while Creswell was chanting 'one, two, three, four'. The timing was impeccable and an air of disgust swept across the faces of the jury members.

'Creswell stopped his car at the Bracken Road. A paramedic got out of their vehicle to find Katie Simpson in the passenger seat of the defendant's car. They noticed that Miss Simpson was only wearing underwear on her bottom half. She wasn't breathing and had no heartbeat. They noticed that she had reddening to her neck and a slight indentation as if something had been placed around it, said Magee.

The jury were told that the ambulance drove on to hospital, leaving police on the roadside to speak to Creswell, conversations that were picked up on the body cameras, footage that would be shown in the courtroom. As the screen was readied for the video footage Creswell shifted uneasily in his seat. Gone was the confidence he had exuded in earlier appearances and even at the beginning of the day. While he had seen the book of evidence and knew the Crown's case against him, hearing his own voice and seeing his own image made everything far more real and far more stark.

In the first clip shown to the jury, Creswell stands on the side of the road as an ambulance stands in the distance. The video was fast forwarded to where police asked him about where the incident had happened and, the jury were told, that was the first time he gave the wrong address. In a second clip, Magee told jurors, Creswell is back at the hospital but is wearing different clothes. The footage played showed him calmer as he stated his name as Jonathan James Creswell, date of birth 23 January 1988, address '4 Gortnessy Woods or Meadows', wrong for a second time . . . 'We are not there that long,' he tells the officer.

Confirm to me who lives in the house, the police officer asks him. 'Myself, my other half Christina Simpson, Katie Simpson, my wee son and my wee daughter . . . Katie Simpson is my wee sister-in-law,' Creswell says, continuing:

I took Michael and Sandra to my mum's and I just looked in the door and eh, I just said I'm going to leave them down to my mum's and she [Katie] said 'All right, I'll see you later.' Then Sandra went over to her and shouted 'bye Katie' and I could hear her say 'bye Sandra'. I went down the road not a care in the world and I went back up and Hayley Robb was about to meet me at the house . . . And then that was all right. I was chatting to her and I went in the door. I'm actually on the phone and I'm chatting and ehm, ehm she said the length of time she was away and I looks up and I see Katie there and I'm like 'What are you doing?' It looked like she was acting the eejit like, her face was touching the wood. And then I knew and I started screaming and running and I held the phone and I lifted her and I shouted, 'Ring the police or ambulance, Katie has hung herself.' The wee girl was flapping and I got her and I didn't know how heavy and I eventually got her . . . I was trying to loosen it first, and then I couldn't and I couldn't get her up high enough and she was making noise and I'm doing everything and undoing it and I breathe into her mouth but sure it was coming out her nose but I could hear something . . . I had to try and carry her. I was trailing her into the car. Her hair and everything was everywhere and she was just flapping and she was blue and her wee tongue was green. And I started driving and I should have kept driving. And then I don't know . . .'

The jury were shown CCTV of Creswell's and Robb's cars pulling into the driveway at Gortnessy after the ambulance had collected Katie. Magee told them: 'Hayley Robb will tell you they arrived at the same time and Creswell told her he was going to take a shower, not just any shower, a cold one. He was going to take a cold one as he didn't want the police to know he had taken a shower. Are they actions of a concerned friend preoccupied by the terrible suicide? Or are they the actions of a cold and calculating killer? Robb will tell you he asked her to take his clothes and wash them, something she did. Then you will also hear at some point Creswell ordered her to clean up the blood. Why? Was this housekeeping? He gave her his clothes, then the two made their way to Altnagelvin in Robb's car.'

Robb, Magee told the jury, was initially not forthcoming about what had occurred. Her image, dressed in leggings and a blue vest coat, was next to be seen by the court as she spoke to officers saying that she'd met Creswell at the house and he 'literally just came out and we went'.

Finally, the bodycam footage of Creswell in the back of the patrol car shows him describing the noose he said he had found Katie hanging from: a 'black thing' with a metal clip on it which he described as like something from a bag.

Asked about Katie's mood, Creswell replied: 'Like she was just a hard worker . . . a hard worker. At times she is high and at times she is low . . . Oh my God, she never expressed suicidal tendencies . . . No, she is not on medication . . . She was saying a while back, she was tired and in the last week or two she had extra strong caffeine super pills . . . She doesn't drink that much . . . . I said if you are tired, rest a bit . . . She has her craic . . . But there is deffo no drugs. She doesn't smoke . . . She likes a drink but not mental but she loves it . . . During hunting season she would be at the hip flask flat out . . . She had a few drinks on Saturday night.' The mention of Saturday night was a reference to the earlier opening of the prosecution that events that night had led to her murder. On the video Creswell insisted that Katie had never tried to self-harm but he did manage to claim she had been trampled the day before by a horse.

'She rides horses and she is a good rider and a very hardy girl ... A tough girl ... She had broken her back before and she wouldn't wait for an ambulance. She got into the car and made me drive her here. She kept walking in with a broken back. So she is tough ... Yesterday her own horse galloped off and she still had the head collar and he trampled over her a bit. There were bruises on her.' Asked if Katie had a boyfriend, Creswell said she didn't.

The opening was powerful and the use of Creswell's voice and images on the screen almost brought the days around Katie's murder to life. In the dock his head hung low and he had adopted an almost foetal position. Closing for the day, the jury were reminded not to read anything about the case and not to discuss it with anyone. They were told to return the following morning. They'd been sworn in the previous day and had been chosen from a jury panel of 73. Judge Neil Rafferty KC had told them that the trial was expected to last between four and six weeks, that 70 people would be giving evidence and that among the locations that would be mentioned were horse yards in Northern Ireland and one in Donegal. Still on bail, Creswell was dismissed for the day and, wearing jeans and a blue jumper, he met with his legal team for consultation before heading home for the night.

Tanya Fowles was at home in Armagh, forced to attend court remotely because of a positive test for Covid. She was expecting the opening of the trial to be interesting, but she couldn't have imagined how dramatic and powerful the case against Creswell would be. She shut her link into the courtroom and started to write her story for a number of different publications that were interested in her copy. Earlier that week, something strange had happened but she had almost put it out of her mind as she pored over the details of the case, many of which she had known but had been unable to report because they were now under court privilege. It was a Tuesday and she knew she was in for a busy week.

There was this other little thing that had happened and it involved a letter that came into the office for me. I was at home that week because I had Covid. This letter arrived on the Monday morning in the *Impartial Reporter* and I got a text from one of my colleagues in work about it. They were concerned because I'm forever getting solicitors' letters and it might have been important to open it before I could make it back to the office. One of my colleagues actually texted, saying 'I don't think this is a solicitor, ha ha.' So I said look I've Covid I can't make it so she says well we will stick it in the post for you. I sort of forgot about it as soon as the trial got under way because it was unbelievable the detail that we had got from the opening speech alone. There was a sense that this is going to be a hard one for Creswell to get out of. There was a kind of confidence in the room.

Abi Lyle waited for the copy to drop online so she could read every detail of what had been said about Creswell and the prosecution case against him. She'd have liked to have been in court to hear it for herself and to see him again for the first time in over ten years, but the timing couldn't have been worse for her. Since she'd moved to the UK Abi had prospered in more ways than one. Her work had given her a love for and a skill in the sport of individual dressage and Abi had proved herself to be so good that she was on the brink of being chosen for the Irish Olympic team. The team was set to be picked during an event in Germany and would be ratified later in the summer by the Olympic Federation of Ireland. While the Olympics was always a dream for Abi, competing in the stunning surrounds of the Palais de Versailles in Paris would be like the cherry on the cake. Abi hadn't heard anything from the PSNI in the months leading up to the trial, so she hoped that nothing would happen that would clash with her work. Then the letter arrived.

'As the trial approached she had got this letter to say she had to make herself available at Derry courthouse,' said Rachel. 'She was like: "What? I can't go, I'm in Germany." So then she had a consultation with the state's senior counsel on the Friday beforehand and he said to her that she wouldn't be called until May and didn't need to be there from the beginning. So then Monday 22 April was the jury selection, Tuesday was the opening,' said Rachel. 'On Wednesday morning I was at my desk and the phone went and it was Abi and she said the police have just phoned me . . . He's dead.'

CHAPTER 13

A SUICIDE

The news that Rachel and Abi had to digest had already reverberated around Coleraine courtroom hours earlier when a strange delay that morning had become the subject of much whispering. It was 24 April 2024 and journalists, lawyers and some of the witnesses due to give evidence were prepared for a second day of what they believed would be sensational evidence against Creswell and of course an idea of how he was going to defend himself, which would follow on from the prosecution's opening. There are often unexplained delays in courtrooms, particularly when links to the court have to be set up for reporters and other interested parties who can't be there in person. But there was a sense that something was different that morning and very soon the phones started to hop. Waiting online for the case to begin, Tanya Fowles got a text from a contact. 'Creswell has been found dead.' By mid-morning a police officer attended the court and told the jury that Creswell had been found dead at 9am that morning and that his identity had been confirmed by a family member. Then they were dismissed and told they could go home.

Later, small details about Creswell's death and the discovery of his body by mum Donna were revealed when evidence was given that he had been bailed to an address at Brunswick Road and that a prison officer, then working for the PSNI, had attended a call that someone was in a hysterical state. When the female officer attended she realised that the deceased was Creswell – she had had dealings with him at Maghaberry Prison when she'd worked there and when he was serving a brief sentence for his attacks on Abi Lyle. No pulse could be found and he was pronounced dead at the house. On a mantelpiece lay a letter that would later be described as a mini-autobiography, blaming all the women in his life for his downfall. Taking no responsibility for his own demise, he blamed lies, deceit and jealousy for his position in front of the court the day before, when the case against him, including the evidence that would be given by Robb and others, had been laid out. Despite the fact that his death would leave the women facing justice alone, he insinuated their treachery had caused him despair. He died as he had lived, blaming others for his demise and his failings and trying to control the narrative until the very end.

In Belfast Rachel Lyle was at first speechless as Abi's words started to sink in. Her sister was at the brink of something enormous in her career and an opportunity she might never get again, but Jonathan Creswell had been like a ghost from her past, always dragging her back when she tried to forget him:

I think we were both frightened. But then we both said 'I'm glad'. And I went outside to get some air and I sat with her on the phone for ages and we sort of talked it through and we were like 'right well it's okay' because I was like 'you can feel happy that he's dead and I'm happy that he's dead'. And once we said that it was so much easier to deal with it. It was like a monster was dead. It took us a while to kind of get there. I was out there in tears crying and then she was competing the next day in Germany and this was to be chosen for the Olympic team. So she is there and she is up to high doh and I then go down to Victoria and I'm running around thinking that all the women of this country are safer and it is because of women like Tanya and Nuala and Abi. I was crying around the park and I texted Tanya and, I was like you are the reason, one of the reasons, why everyone is so much safer now. And I was ringing later on and voice messaging her and thanking her and telling her that everyone would be safer because she was so brave.'

The following day Abi issued a statement to the BBC. She expressed her sympathies with Katie's family and said: 'Although it is a shame we didn't get to see Jonathan Creswell face his crimes and be brought to justice, I take a lot of solace in the fact that he will never be able to hurt another person again.'

A letter arrived at Tanya's home two days after Creswell died. 'It came to me by Friday and I opened it up and there was this typed letter. So I started reading.' It was headed in block capitals 'KATIE SIMPSON MURDER TRIAL.'

Underneath the writer had typed a name and accused that person of lying to police, of being involved on the day that Katie Simpson had died, of letting pieces of information slip, admitting their role in helping Creswell cover up the death and even helping to lift Katie's unconscious body from the house at Gortnessy Meadows.

Tanya considered the information. At the opening of the trial the jury had been shown CCTV footage of Christina leaving the house at 6am and later Rose leaving and driving away in a car described as Creswell's. Then Creswell could be seen leaving in Katie's car, returning to the house and leaving again. While the CCTV managed to pick up activities at the cars and in the driveway of the home it hadn't captured what had happened at the door or Katie being put into the passenger seat. Whoever wrote the letter had spelled Creswell's name incorrectly, but that didn't mean much as it was an easy name to insert a second 's' into.

The letter continued and now turned to discuss Rose De Montmorency Wright and her involvement with Creswell and his crew: 'Rose had lived with Cresswell, Nina, Katie and the kids for quite some time and was fully involved in the family and horse aspect and how the family dynamics worked. Katie and Rose shared a bedroom but she would often sleep on the sofa as she had the night before Katie's assault.' Tanya scribbled down a note for herself that the writer had failed to use the word 'murder'. It went on: 'Rose was aware of the abuse and that Katie had just started a new relationship. Katie had divulged to Rose she was worried about the consequences if Cresswell were to become aware of her new boyfriend and had asked her boyfriend not to come to the yard and cause friction at home.'

While Tanya knew that Rose had told officers and others that Katie wasn't in a relationship, she was also aware that police believed that the pair had been together for a short time before her death and that he had secretly visited her the night before. It didn't make sense that she had told Rose about it. Rose also knew that McCloskey had been at the house in Gortnessy in the aftermath of Katie's murder and had met Paul Lusby there when he came to find out what had happened.

The letter went on to make further accusations about Rose and threats that Creswell had allegedly made to her if she revealed details of things that had happened at Gortnessy Meadows.

Rose's story was she didn't return to the house but went shopping in Tesco and then slept in her car. Why wouldn't she go back to Newtownards where her family home was after her best friend had apparently tried to take her own life? Was she so traumatised or controlled by Cresswell and those were her instructions from him?

The letter continued:

After Katie's death and funeral Rose continued to live with Cresswell and once the police started to investigate Katie's murder, both Rose and Cresswell were questioned. Cresswell then told Rose to 'get out of here, they're coming to get me'. Rose lived with them for quite some time working with Cresswell every day, plenty of time to indoctrinate or perhaps you could say brainwash her young influential brain and with time this distorted her memory and true understanding of what she had done. She is quite unconcerned and blasé with regard to any feelings she may have towards Katie or the whole court proceedings.

Once she moved to England she kept in contact via two phones. She used one for family and friends and the other to keep in contact with Cresswell, Robinson etc. . . . Katie's phone went missing, did Rose know anything about that as she was at the assault site just after it happened, although this information may not be known by the authorities.

Rose has told so many lies she isn't sure what [is] the truth. She only pleaded guilty as Hayley Robb had and forced her and Robinson to finally admit their part in the whole sordid affair. Hayley Robb seems to be the only one with a moral compass out of the three. My information was that now that she had pleaded guilty Rose may not have to go into the witness box? Hopefully this is misleading and the truth can come out when Rose, Hayley and Jill are in the witness box. They were all so controlled by a narcissistic man with previous experience of strangulation of loved ones, they can't see the wood from the trees.

I want justice to be served and all those involved to serve their time.

Thank you.

Tanya said, 'So it was significant because it had been posted before the trial started. I thought the right thing to do was alert the police even though they had been so useless from the beginning. But I felt I had an obligation all the same. I mean the trial was over, Johnny had killed himself and I thought well this is what I need to do as a citizen. Never again! That was another palaver.' Tanya tried to do some detective work herself. The address on the envelope was handwritten, but the letter was typed. While some of the content was plausible, some was not.

'So I reported it on the Friday night and the next morning I got a phone call from the Major Investigation Team. They said they needed to take a statement and collect the letter. I made it quite clear that I wasn't happy about police conduct in the original investigation but the woman said she was independent of that and had a supervisor who needed to see the letter. And I eventually said that was fine. I'd tested clear for Covid so I went that morning to meet with them.

I had been careful. Once I'd taken the letter out and saw Rose's name on it I'd grabbed a pair of gloves because I didn't want to get fingerprints on it. I'd put it in poly pocket things and brought it all in with me and then they took a statement. Afterwards they phoned me to thank me for meeting them and that was it. I didn't hear a word. When I followed it up and asked what happened they said they looked at it and it wasn't credible. I had my suspicions where it came from and what the purpose of it was. I was fully convinced that it was someone close to Creswell trying to manipulate the situation and pin the blame on Rose, planting her right in the middle of it.

But Tanya didn't have long to wait before the PSNI that she had struggled against to launch a murder probe became the headline itself. Days after Creswell's death the Policing Board was told that officers who had probed Katie's death had 'committed misconduct'. Alliance Party Policing Board member Nuala McAllister told the PSNI Chief Constable Jon Boutcher: 'The death of Jonathan Creswell was a massive blow to justice for Katie and her family and loved ones. I just want to ask to ensure that Katie's legacy is that this never happens again to another woman and we rid society of violence against women and girls.'

Boutcher gave an overview of the complaints:

A number of departments and branches who responded, including detectives of various ranks, carried out initial enquiries, including during the weekend of August 14, when information was raised with us around a concern about the causes of Katie's death . . . But, in effect, due to people raising concerns about Creswell and his behaviour between August and December [2020], there were a number that led to a reassessment of what had happened. In January of 2021, Creswell was determined to be a suspect in the murder of Ms Simpson. In March, he was arrested and prosecuted.

There has been a Police Ombudsman's investigation and I have been in touch with the ombudsman this week in regards to that investigation, to ensure that any information we have about our response is properly examined so that we understand any lessons to be learned . . . We have a circa 1,400-page report from the ombudsman which has identified officers having committed misconduct – not gross misconduct or criminal – and that misconduct process is now under way through our professional standards department, under the stewardship of the Deputy Chief Constable. These events will be further examined, I suspect, through an inquest into Ms Simpson's death.

PSNI Temporary Assistant Chief Constable Davy Beck added:

For confirmation and clarity, I can confirm that, while Katie Simpson was being treated in hospital, a member of the public did contact police with concerns regarding the incident, suggesting that it may not have been a suicide attempt. This was flagged with Criminal Investigation Department officers and, as a result of that, a forensic post-mortem examination was directed and a CID detective attended that post-mortem, which was conducted on August 11, to help and advise the pathologist. The coroner still has to direct an inquest, so it would not be appropriate to expand on the pathologist's finding at this time, it was accepted by police at the time that the incident was non-suspicious. Clearly there was other information in the weekend that followed, of August 14, that required further examination.

Eleven days after he died Creswell was buried in the presence of just two mourners at Ballyoan Cemetery in Derry's Waterside. The man and the woman dressed completely in black left a large arrangement of white flowers on his grave. Shortly afterwards disgusted relatives of loved ones buried close suggested they wanted Creswell's body dug up and moved.

CHAPTER 14

THE WOMEN

It was a bright and sunny June morning in 2024 and the courthouse in Derry convened shortly after 10am. For many, this was the first time they had seen the three women in the dock outside the social media shots of Jonathan Creswell's circle of women. Hayley Robb looked far less glamorous than she did in the pictures she had posed for with Katie Simpson. Gone was the thick kohl eyeliner, the smoky eyeshadow and the bright red lips. Instead she looked wholesome, awkward and ashamed. Jill Robinson, older than the other two, was dressed in a tan tweed coat with her blonde hair tied back. Rose De Montmorency Wright wore an ill-fitting grey suit which she pulled at repeatedly. She had a childlike demeanour and seemed distracted and giddy. Robinson sat in the middle, and while she and De Montmorency Wright chatted a little as they waited for the hearing to start, Robb sat a slight distance away, an outsider in every way. She was the whistleblower, the one who had broken rank and collapsed Creswell's carefully constructed house of cards. Following her interviews in May and June 2021 after Creswell was arrested and charged with Katie's murder, Hayley had agreed to become a state witness at his trial. In fact, police were convinced that without her their case wouldn't have been half as strong, but still she had to face criminal charges herself.

The PPS had considered her role in Katie's death and decided that she had misled police from the moment of her arrival at the hospital with Creswell, had removed the clothing that may have contained critical scientific material capable of establishing how Katie had died, and had cleaned up the blood in the house. She'd also failed to disclose that Creswell had taken a cold shower and had told her he had 'given Katie a hiding' the night before. The Crown argued that had Hayley been honest with them at the hospital the detection of foul play would have been inevitable and her dishonesty had ultimately accentuated the harm suffered by Katie's relatives. The Crown also argued that, while they would use her as a witness, her evidence had not led to Creswell's arrest but it was important.

Her plea of guilty in December were to 3 offences; one related to withholding information and the other two counts were for perverting the course of justice by cleaning the blood and washing the clothes. Robb accepted that she failed without reasonable excuse to give information to the police within reasonable time, did not know or believe Creswell had murdered Katie but thought he'd assaulted her and that she was aware that while police would be investigating the circumstances of Katie's death, she knew that Creswell did not want police to know about the assault. The prosecution also accepted when she did eventually provide an account that she did so to the best of her abilities and that she had done what Creswell had asked her to do. This was followed quickly by a similar plea from Robinson in January 2022, as Creswell remained on bail, and then by Rose De Montmorency Wright.

Robinson had not made any statements to police over the course of the initial investigation, but in June 2021 she said she'd known Creswell a long time, had been in a relationship with him for two years and had been friends ever since. Creswell had been in touch from prison, she admitted, but she hadn't complained that he controlled or assaulted her. She'd admitted to the meeting at the layby near the Foyle Bridge the day that Katie had been taken to hospital and said he'd been crying in the car but insisted that nothing of any significance was imparted at that time. When pressed, she said she'd reassured Creswell when he said: 'youse think I did this', saying to him that he 'doted on' Katie. She couldn't remember him saying he would claim she was trampled by a horse to explain her injuries. She told her own story about washing his clothes – Hayley having said it wasn't unusual, and that she didn't know they belonged to Creswell. She told police that she often washed riding-related items for him and hadn't given it any thought. Jill had delivered the clothes back to Donna Creswell's home after washing them. Police put it to her that Johnny, Donna, her partner and Christina were there at the time. She confirmed that but said first that nobody had asked her any questions about them or where they came from. She said that she didn't believe anyone in the house even noticed her bringing them back but eventually, in the same interview, she had said she'd told Christina that she washed them saying she didn't ask why. Within seconds of stating that, she said she wasn't sure what she told Christina about the clothes as she couldn't remember.

In October that year Robinson had been interviewed again when further aspects of an account given by Christina Simpson were put to her. Christina had told police that she'd had a conversation with Robinson about Creswell's admission that he had assaulted Katie, but she denied this conversation ever took place. She admitted deleting some messages on her phone but said there was nothing sinister in that. The prosecution concluded that

Robinson had destroyed potentially incriminating evidence when she and Hayley washed his clothes. In January 2022, as Creswell remained on bail, Robinson pleaded guilty to one offence of perverting the course of justice but the basis of her plea was that she did not know that Creswell had murdered Katie but that she had washed his clothes with Hayley Robb.

Rose had been even more difficult to crack. In January 2021, when the murder inquiry was launched, she had given a statement insisting that Katie had had a fall from a horse before she died, an incident she claimed to have witnessed. In a second statement she identified a mobile phone that wasn't Katie's and said Robb had cleaned up blood at the house. Rose had gone to work in England two weeks before Creswell's arrest and in August 2021 she returned for an interview, insisting that everything she had said before was true. She said Creswell was a close friend and someone that she looked up to but denied that he had any kind of hold over her. She said that she had never been in a sexual relationship with him and knew nothing of anything between him and Katie. She had insisted to officers that she spoke to Katie when she arrived home 10 minutes after Creswell on the night of the Lurgan show. Katie, she said, had told her she'd been trampled by Nelson. When she got up the following morning she claimed she brought tea to both and that Creswell was in the children's bedroom and Katie in her own. De Montmorency Wright said she'd left in a rush as she was late. Later, when she was at work, she had heard that Katie had been found hanging. She said she phoned and texted both Katie's and Creswell's numbers and eventually a woman answered, who she believed to be Katie. She said she rang Christina to tell her that her sister was fine but later Robinson told Rose that was not the case.

De Montmorency Wright said that her comments about Katie attempting suicide previously were in the context of believing she had taken her own life. She insisted that the accident with the horse had happened, even saying Katie had videoed it and later deleted it from her phone. After a period of time she had admitted to police that when Katie was in hospital, Creswell had told her he'd hit her with a stick around the ankles. When asked why she hadn't told police that before, she said she was worried it was 'going to cause harm'. At one point she said that she'd said certain things because she was trying to 'have Johnny's back'. She had claimed to have no recollection of a two-minute phone call with Creswell before he dropped his children to his mother's house.

Interviewed again in October 2021, De Montmorency Wright had told police she didn't want to comment, but the prosecution had decided that her silence had been a criminal offence. Her failure to mention critical facts in her witness statements, in particular that Creswell had admitted to beating Katie in the lead-up to her assault, had contributed to derailing the police investigation.

Hours after Robinson had changed her position, Rose De Montmorency Wright followed suit pleading guilty to one count of withholding information. Like Robb and Robinson, her plea was accepted on the basis that she didn't know Creswell had murdered Katie but believed he'd assaulted her. The prosecution also accepted that De Montmorency Wright withheld information from police but did not recall some aspects of her interactions with Creswell including telephone calls at relevant times on the morning of August 3rd.

All three women had one thing in common on that June morning – they all looked out of place in the dock.

Judge Neil Rafferty KC, cementing his reputation for straight talking and efficiency, took the unusual step of speaking directly to the press before the proceedings began to confirm that all reporting restrictions had been lifted, orders which had at one point afforded the women anonymity. The first order of business was evidence of the discovery of Creswell's body months earlier by a former prison officer from Maghaberry Prison who had gone to the scene as the first responder, arriving to find a hysterical woman and Creswell dead at the end of a noose in the undisclosed bail address where he had been living for months. The women in the dock listened intently, unfamiliar with what would happen next.

The prosecution then opened the case with a bluntness that would bring anyone thinking the girls didn't belong in these surroundings back to earth. The case, it said, surrounded the murder of Katie Simpson. It was the Crown's case that she had died at the hands of Jonathan Creswell when he strangled and killed her during a sexual liaison and that the women now standing before Judge Rafferty had made efforts to cover up what he had done as he tried to make her death look like a suicide. The women in the dock had interfered with evidence in order to protect Creswell from being suspected of a role in Katie's death and yet they stood alone now to face justice in front of members of her family and the media from across the UK and Ireland. The defendants, the court heard, had admitted their guilt, but only on the basis that they did not know the truth of what had occurred or exactly what Creswell had done; they only knew he had assaulted Katie and they didn't want the PSNI to know that when they were invest-igating her suicide.

Robb, the court heard, was first to plead guilty. She admitted that she had cleaned blood from a banister in the house and had taken the clothes Creswell had been wearing to be washed. Robb was not only the first to admit what she'd done; she had later offered to turn King's evidence against Creswell. Robinson later agreed that she had washed the clothes with Robb, after she'd arrived with them in her car, while De Montmorency Wright accepted she'd withheld information but could not help with details of telephone calls she'd had with him in his cover-up of the murder – she said she could not recall them.

Details of Katie's liaison with Shane McCloskey and their text messages to one another was read out to the court, and the group's activities in the 24 hours before her death, including the show in Lurgan, were laid out. During the course of that evidence De Montmorency Wright shook her head in disagreement, often looking at Jill Robinson for support, in particular when the court heard that after the show Creswell and Katie had travelled in the rear of the horse box to Robinson's yard in Omagh.

The court heard the timeline of Creswell's movements as he headed across the border to Lifford with Katie, the pair's arrival back home in Derry at 12:25am, and the movements around the house the next morning. The calls to Robb, the 999 message and Creswell's meeting with the medical personnel as he pretended to carry out CPR were recounted. Creswell's use of Robb as his alibi witness was clear, and in the dock she dropped her head and listened intently about how she had gone with him to the hospital.

The details of Katie's injuries made it seem strange that her death had been accepted as a suicide by the original investigation team. She'd ultimately died, the court heard, after being rendered unconscious by brain injuries. Over the days in the hospital, as she clung to life on a machine, some of the bruises on her limbs had gone purple and blue, but they suggested she'd been struck by a rod or a firm strap. A bruise on her forearm showed similar patterning. In hospital the post-mortem had found a mark on her neck that suggested some form of ligature, but the marks were not consistent with hanging. Grip marks were still evident on the back of her right thigh and there was evidence of sexual assault. The injuries to her face, hands, shin and thighs were made with the repeated use of a weapon, or there had been multiple attacks over many hours, the court was told. 'She simply couldn't have died in the way he suggested,' the court heard. 'The DNA gathered assisted the prosecution case that he [Creswell] had intercourse with her and raped her before death. The court was also in receipt of evidence of his behaviour at the wake and funeral.'

The statements made by Hayley Robb were detailed. In her statement on 2 March 2021, seven months after Katie's death, and when the fresh team of detectives had arrested Creswell, she had told PSNI officers that he made a 20-minute phone call to her during her journey from Banbridge as he got the kids into the car. She said he'd phoned her again on the way back and they talked about horse sales. During that first interview she insisted that she and Creswell were just friends, but on 17 March, after he had been charged with murder, she admitted they had been in a sexual relationship for nine or ten years, that he was very controlling, and that he would take her phone if he suspected she was in contact with other men. She had told the PSNI he'd called her a 'cunt' and a 'whore' for seeing other people, and when she was on a night out and didn't report in to him, he would contact her on Snapchat. On the Monday when Katie was brought to Altnagelvin Hospital, she said, she was due to meet him for sex, but she said she knew nothing about his relationship with Katie. Robb eventually told police that he'd told her he'd hit Katie the night before and, while she was vague about the details, she did state he'd given her a 'hiding'. She told them about the shower he had taken but said she felt that was a normal thing to do and never thought anything more of it. She said he'd asked her to clean the blood as he didn't want Christina finding it. She'd put his clothes in a bag and was told 'not to breathe a word of it'. She went to Jill Robinson's, she said, and she told her about the laundry facility, and afterwards she had taken a few days off work. Eventually she broke down and said Creswell had dragged her into it. She said she was afraid of him because he'd been controlling her and had assaulted her during the sexual relationship, which had continued up until his arrest. She was frightened of him. During a further interview in June she said that she had witnessed him assaulting Christina Simpson.

But the prosecution also said she'd misled police, underplayed her role in the cover-up and her actions meant she had eradicated damning evidence against him. While the Crown acknowledged that she had been due to be called as a witness and had showed genuine remorse for her actions, there was a need to consider the amount of help she had given Creswell. Justice Rafferty, addressing the prosecution, suggested that people were now much more alert to coercive control. He asked: 'You seem to be suggesting that coercive control is a modus operandi? Is it just part of the facts of the case? Or is it a mitigating factor?'

Jill Robinson, the judge was told, had never made any suggestion that Creswell was in control of her and had said she was not afraid of him. The statements made by Rose De Montmorency Wright seemed totally confused, given how events had turned out. Her relationship with Creswell, she insisted to police, was not sexual.

De Montmorency Wright's legal team, under Mr O'Donoghue, said his client was 19 years of age at the time and was a 'young lady' who had been well educated and brought up in a family that was as 'far away from appearing before a criminal court' as anyone could imagine. The fact she was caught up in the 'incident' was a matter of deep regret and remorse to her. 'She never intended to get involved in anything like this. It shows the unfettered control he [Creswell] had over the lives of young women. At the time of the offence he was in his early 30s and had talents in his own way to create a web of relationships over the years' and a very high degree of control over young ladies. 'My client was undoubtedly one,' he said. 'One of the features of controlling relationships is that those being controlled can't see it or acknowledge it and this is a feature of her involvement with Creswell. My client would not be before this court save for false loyalties and failing to do the right thing as one is brought up to do.'

He continued:

It all goes against the grain of this young lady and she now acknowledges that is a criminal offence. But for the nature of this relationship, she would not have been before the court. She has gone on to work and has gone on to live a life with no suggestion of any criminality or wrongdoing. There is no suggestion she was involved in planning or preparing this crime and that is why I come back to fake loyalties and misconceived loyalties against a background of control. She has had an exemplary life and is a hardworking young lady. This has had a significant impact on her personally and professionally. She has a love of horses and has sought to pursue a career – and that is a material consequence – outside of Northern Ireland. She is now working elsewhere, outside of this jurisdiction and has an otherwise trustworthy character. She has shown appropriate empathy and understanding for what has happened. She lost a dear and valued friend.

Robb, the court heard, was told by Creswell what to do and she was a victim of his controlling and violent behaviour. The prosecution accepted that she had led an otherwise blameless life and had never intended to be involved with criminality. She was filled with genuine remorse and regret for what had happened and she had made formal complaints of assault against Creswell. Just yards away from her, Rose looked around the courtroom and yawned.

Mitigating arguments for Robinson heard that she fully accepted her guilt and responsibility, but had a misguided loyalty to Creswell. She had conducted herself in an 'exemplary fashion' over the course of the case against her and had adhered to bail conditions. She was at risk of losing her good character – something, the court heard, that individuals hold with great pride as they get older. 'The impact of the offence is that it will be a stain for the rest of her life.' Nobody spoke as Justice Rafferty released the women on continuing bail and told them to be back in his court within weeks for sentencing. Outside, each disappeared into cars with family members and were driven away.

Later that month they were back to hear their fate. Justice Neil Rafferty KC entered the courtroom quickly, took his seat and looked down at the three accused, together but alone with their own thoughts. Their families sat behind them, towards the back of the court, anxious and attentive. To their right and left, towards the judge's bench, members of the media took their place in elevated seating for what would be the final chapter in a story of murder and betrayal. But first it was time to remember who was at the heart of it.

'I will start these sentencing remarks the way I always start sentencing remarks of this kind, by first referring to the victim statements,' Justice Rafferty said in a crystal clear voice. He had, he said, received numerous reports about Katie and the impact of her death on those who knew her, in particular her family. Noeleen Simpson, Katie's mother, had described being devastated when she was told that her daughter had taken her own life but said if any of the women in the dock had been truthful she would have been better able to comfort Katie and would never have let Creswell near her bedside as she died.

Christina Simpson, who'd shared her murderous lover with her youngest sibling, told the judge that the void left by Katie's loss would never be filled. Rebecca Simpson described her sister as 'imperfect and perfect', adding that she had lost faith in the world and in people. 'I have become fearful of what the future holds for my girls,' she wrote. 'My daughter was born two weeks after Katie died, and I feel devastated that she will never get to meet her.' Katie's grandparents, Colm and Angela Mullan, and her aunt and uncle, Conor and Colleen McConville, had given the judge a picture, he said, of a hardworking horsewoman who was kind to younger relatives and full of fun. Apart from her family, Judge Rafferty said, Katie had friends who'd written their own victim impact statements.

It is clear from everything that I have read that Katie Simpson was a fun, loving, caring, talented horsewoman who was loved deeply not only by her family but also her many friends which she had. Her loss, and the circumstances of it, have left very many people shocked, devastated and angry that her passing has so cruelly deprived her of the bright future which she undoubtedly would have had. I take the time to address the victim statements in cases like this because victims often listen to sentencing remarks which deal with defendants and mistakenly think the sentencing is 'all about them'. It isn't. However, any proper sentencing exercise requires an examination of the guidelines and the defendants' circumstances, and it is to that exercise that I now turn.

In the body of the court, Hayley Robb smoothed down her top while Rose De Montmorency Wright turned her head to the back of the courtroom, where her parents sat.

Following his assault on Katie Simpson, Creswell tried to make her condition and her subsequent death look like a suicide. Together with others, he disposed of and interfered with evidence with the inevitable consequence of misleading those investigating her death. Accounts were provided by Creswell and these defendants which were intended to and had the effect of protecting Creswell from being suspected of having a role in her death. Mr Creswell himself created a fiction, pretending to others he had found Katie, hanging in a stairwell from a strap, claiming she had taken her own life. These defendants did not know the truth about how she had met her death. However, they ascribed to and were complicit in his conspiracy of silence with regards to a number of critical facts and in Robb and Robinson's case engaged in positive acts, the result of which was to mislead those trying to get to the truth of what had happened to Katie Simpson.

All three defendants, the judge said, had pleaded guilty, which was of value; and Robb had been due to be a witness, her evidence being so important that it would have featured in the opening day of Creswell's trial.

Turning to the media, the judge clarified that each woman had the same basis for their pleas – that they believed that Creswell had assaulted Katie prior to her alleged suicide and that they did not know or believe he had murdered her. Of Robb he said: 'The defendant was aware that the police would be investigating the circumstances of Katie's death and was aware that Creswell did not want police to know about his assault on Katie or to find the blood on clothes in the course of their investigation.' Saying her guilty plea merited significant credit, he also pointed out that she was the first defendant to engage with the prosecution. A month later, in January 2024, Jill Robinson had followed suit, also pleading guilty on the basis that she didn't know or believe that Creswell had murdered Katie. The same day, in the immediate aftermath of Robinson's plea, Rose De Montmorency Wright had also pleaded guilty and the prosecution had accepted that she didn't recall calls with Creswell at times on the morning of 3 August. 'The central theme of all three basis of plea documents is that all three defend-ants acted upon Creswell's lie that he had "given Katie a hiding" the night before he claimed to have found her and that she had attempted suicide. That is to say, the basis upon which I must sentence all three is that they did not know or believe that Creswell had in reality murdered Katie Simpson,' he said.

He paid tribute to other witnesses who had come forward, in particular Abi Lyle, whose statement was 'the most compelling picture of Creswell'. He had subjected her to 'choking and stran-gulation', which was then a stand-alone criminal offence known as 'non-fatal strangulation', an offence that hadn't existed at the time of those attacks. Statistically, he pointed out, a man who engages in a non-fatal strangulation is 800 per cent more likely to kill a partner. 'The number of witnesses; the volume of evidence they give; and the detail and contents of these statements create an irresistible conclusion that Jonathan Creswell was a skilled and predatory abuser who regarded women under his influence as simply there to be used and abused for his own ends including his sexual gratification.'

Robb stood for sentence. Aged 30, she had returned to live with her parents and had attempted to move forward with her life, but had been so aggressively doorstepped by the media in the run-up to her trial that she had had to see a mental health professional. She had also run the Belfast Marathon to raise money for domestic abuse victims. Robinson was also on her feet. She had taken a degree in geography at Queen's University Belfast and had worked in various stables before meeting Creswell, five years younger than her. They were in a relationship for two years but, unlike Robb, she had denied that he was physically violent to her. De Montmorency Wright had been only 16 when she'd met Creswell, the judge said, noting she was 18 when she went to live with him.

Despite their clean criminal records and low risk of re-offending, what the women had done was still a serious matter, the judge said.

I am satisfied that the offences to which all three defendants have pleaded guilty are serious and that they cross the custo-dial threshold . . . I also consider it appropriate to suspend the sentence in each case given the one-off nature of the offending and the absence of any material criminal record on the part of each of these defendants. I do not consider it necessary to impose an immediate custodial term which will significantly jeopardise each of their abilities to contribute to society either in their employment or by way of their family responsibilities. I am entirely satisfied that but for the agency and control of Jonathan Creswell none of them would ever have stood in a dock; the using of them by Creswell was cynical and exploitative – for example, I am entirely satisfied, and, indeed, it was the prosecution case, that the telephone call to Hayley Robb on the morning of Katie's death was to ensure that Creswell could use her as a witness to him 'finding' Katie's body. A further factor in Robb's case is that she had made a statement after her plea and had asserted a desire to 'turn King's evidence'. Her evidence was a significant plank in the prosecution narrative. For all of these reasons, I am satisfied that the sentences in this case should be suspended for a period of two years. Accordingly, I impose the following sentences . . .

He imposed a two-year sentence on Robb, a 16-month term for Robinson and eight months for De Montmorency Wright before warning all three: 'I am obliged by law to explain what a suspended sentence is. If you commit any further offences punishable by imprisonment within the next two years you will go to jail for that offence and this sentence will be put into operation.'

With that, the women were dismissed and the courtroom started to empty, but the story was far from over. A catalogue of policing failures were set to make for a shocking file, one that echoed a botched investigation from 1993, which had been made into a TV drama starring one of Northern Ireland's most celebrated actors, James Nesbitt, in the role of murderous dentist Colin Howell.

Chapter 15

The Fallout

The Police Ombudsman's report into the flawed police investigation into the murder of Katie Simpson makes for grim and frightening reading. It reveals a catalogue of errors that saw a crass murder cover-up almost go unpunished. The report is yet to be published, but thanks to a small army of people, mostly strangers to Katie Simpson, the details in it have been leaked. It is impossible to say whether or not the reasons why Katie was buried as a suicide victim are down to incompetence, but the shocking findings are riddled with missed opportunities that should lead to a full-scale inquiry, as repeatedly called for by Tanya Fowles, into her death and the responses to it.

Katie was just 21 years of age when she died in hospital without regaining consciousness on 10 August 2020. She lay, clinging to life, surrounded by her family and the man who would ultimately be accused of her murder, an act carried out in a fit of violence spurred by a jealous rage. Jonathan Creswell was incensed that the little sister of his partner Christina had spent a night with a young single man whom she fancied and who liked her back. She had been brutally beaten and raped by the time Creswell delivered her to ambulance personnel on the side of the road. Yet for months police treated her death as a suicide, despite multiple reports from people who had independently of one another expressed concern that Creswell was a convicted abuser who had controlled and terrified Katie, and despite the fact that taking her own life was completely out of sync with her character and her hopes for the future.

The Ombudsman's investigation concluded that the police investigation that should have looked into suspicions around her death was hindered by officers who believed Jonathan Creswell's version of events – that Katie's injuries were caused by a horse and were self-inflicted. Despite the fact that concerns were logged by police and, on some occasions, detailed handwritten notes were taken, it took a long time for a murder investigation to be launched, and as a result huge evidential opportunities were missed.

Speaking after the investigation findings were given to the Simpson family, Hugh Hume, the Police Ombudsman Chief Executive, said: 'There appeared to be a general lack of an investigative mindset which contributed to shortcomings in evidence identification and retrieval, scene management and identification, a willingness to accept at face value the accounts from Jonathan Creswell, and ultimately confusion around the ownership of the police investigation.'

The Police Ombudsman investigation concluded that the scene was a major problem when it came to the investigation. No proper or effective searches were carried out in the house at Gortnessy Meadows where Katie died. Officers had arrived there at 9:10am on the morning she was taken to hospital, and a log was opened. House-to-house enquiries were carried out and a CCTV opportunity identified. At 10:25am, records showed, the scene was secured and her car and clothing seized for forensic examination. The ligature was seized and there was a search for a suicide note but none was found. A note said that after discussions with CID it was advised that the family should be contacted to find out what stables had been used over the weekend and to enquire about the fall, but that never happened. At around 4:30pm the log was updated to show that Christina had been spoken to, but less than an hour later the scene was closed and from 4 August until Katie's death on 10 August the investigation responsibility remained with inexperienced officers from the local police taskforce.

One officer, the Ombudsman report found, had an 'ill feeling' about Creswell and a hunch that something was not right; Creswell hadn't gone straight to the hospital and when he had arrived was emotional but swung from sobbing to being very concentrated. He said he'd discussed his doubts with his sergeants, but he'd had no further involvement with the case after that first day.

While it fell short of describing Creswell's car as a second crime scene, the Ombudsman's report said that the searches of it were not satisfactory and while it was seized no log of any search or examination was recorded. The car had been directed to be handed back to Creswell the evening he delivered Katie to the ambulance, but it remained with police until 25 August, when it was searched and two mobile phones were found. It was eventually returned to him in December with no forensic examination ever having taken place. The phones in the car were old ones that had belonged to Katie, but devices she may have been using in the house were not seized and nobody sought to find her current handset, which would have contained the deleted messages between her and Shane McCloskey.

At the hospital, despite concerns of medical staff about her condition, no photographs were taken of her injuries and no blood sampled, despite the fact that the prognosis from the beginning was that she was unlikely to survive. Although her clothing was seized, bloodstains on her underwear were missed, even though advice was given that samples would be reliable for up to seven days.

Intelligence that came in to police while Katie was in hospital and in the aftermath of her death was not appropriately followed up by investigators, the Ombudsman found. Videos of Abi Lyle talking about the abuse she had suffered at the hands of Jonathan Creswell had been viewed by some officers and emails about it exchanged, but no red flag seemed to be raised as a result. On 4 August, a day after she was admitted to hospital, a police officer known as '5' became aware of intelligence from Crimestoppers. This was the first report made by Paul Lusby, who stated that Katie had been living in 'domestic servitude' with Creswell and that he was controlling her and her phone. No further direction or investigative considerations were specified about the information. On 8 August, two days before her death, a member of the public had attended Strand Road PSNI station to report concerns they had in relation to Jonathan Creswell and the way in which Katie was found. Creswell, she reported, was controlling, strict and abusive. This member of the public also questioned why Jonathan Creswell had been allowed to return to the house. The member of the public was dissatisfied with the response they received from PSNI, the Ombudsman found.

On 10 August, the second Crimestoppers tip-off from Lusby was received; this said that Creswell controlled a group of girls and that medical staff were concerned about the circumstances of Katie's death. On 11 August a police officer was asked to share this intelligence with the PSNI's Public Protection Unit. Two days later two further pieces of intelligence came in that there was a belief in the community that she hadn't committed suicide and that she hadn't fallen from a horse. The PSNI Public Protection Unit received the intelligence on 18 August, but still the same mindset existed – that, just as Creswell claimed, Katie had committed suicide. 'It is clear . . . that the intelligence received and available to both LPT [the Local Policing Team] and CID did not change the direction of the investigation,' the report states.

As the weeks wore on officers sought reviews of the case, some raising concerns about the intelligence that was being received and about videos of Abi Lyle found online, but still the case remained with local police and still it was categorised as suicide.

Following Katie's death on 10 August the police log showed that a CID officer did seek clarification around bruising and the post-mortem examination. The officer also highlighted discrepancies around the information provided by Jonathan Creswell and Hayley Robb regarding the telephone calls they made to each other, and inconsistencies in their accounts regarding the horse riding fall and the injuries to Katie's body. However, an officer said that a consultant from the hospital said there was nothing untoward in Katie's toxicology or on her body, and that there were no signs of disturbance at the home or in Katie's vehicle. The same officer did not request any enquiries regarding concerns that had been supposedly raised by the medical staff.

One log suggested prioritising locating Katie's mobile phone to clarify her movements and revisiting witness statements. But while

Creswell had told police that Katie was injured in an accident with a horse, no CCTV was checked or collected and no witnesses were sought who might have seen what happened.

Enquiries could have been made at an early stage about Katie's mobile phone, the Ombudsman points out, and by speaking with family and friends about concerns around her life, but they weren't; and no enquiries were made with medical staff until the case was taken over months later, which meant a number of people who would have been valuable to the investigation were missed.

The police log also recorded one officer speaking to the pathologist on 24 August, who said that the only reason he stated possible hanging as the cause of death was because that was the information he was given. As Katie was alive for seven days after the incident, most bruising would have subsided, the officer reported.

The failure to record a full statement from Paul Lusby in October when he met with a police officer, and the shredding of the detailed notes taken then, was also criticised. Crucially, police had not followed up on one critical piece of CCTV, gathered on 24 August, which could have blown the whole case open. On it were images of Hayley Robb leaving Gortnessy Meadows and placing a bag in the boot of her car, but police didn't follow it up. Other failings highlighted in the report include confusion around the ownership of the investigation. Incredibly, police were updating Creswell on their investigation while also accepting information provided by him. A lack of experience in some police teams, poor entries in the log and limited attempts by officers to respond to Tanya Fowles has also been mentioned in the report. As a result of the investigation breaches of the PSNI Code of

Ethics have been identified, officers have been served with formal written notices and some have been interviewed under misconduct caution.

The report examined the December 2020 meeting of officers from LPT, CID and MIT (the Major Investigation Team) to discuss the investigation into Katie's death. Enquiries completed, evidence obtained and outstanding jobs were noted. An officer stated that there was speculation and anger about the case and it was necessary to establish all evidential information. By 19 January 2021, the Ombudsman found, the ownership of the inquiry was passed on to a new team as a potential homicide. Finally, a police officer had declared the death suspicious and directed that the investigative response should now transfer in its entirety as a potential homicide.

The Ombudsman concluded:

Ownership of the case was initially assigned to an inexperienced officer from a Local Policing Team, despite more experienced officers in local policing, CID and MIT being fully aware that the officer had neither the experience nor the capacity to manage a case of this nature. When concerns were raised early in the investigation, particularly in respect of Jonathan Creswell's history of violent and controlling behaviour, it was the clear duty of those more experienced officers to ensure there was proper supervision, guidance and control. If not for concerns raised by a small number of individuals, both inside and outside the PSNI, there is every likelihood that Katie's death would have been recorded as a suicide. That would have deprived her family and friends of any opportunity for justice, which was ultimately denied them by Creswell's death. It would, however, also have exposed members of the public, particularly young women, to the continued risk posed by Creswell, whose actions, had they gone undetected, may have become increasingly emboldened.

CONCLUSION

Paul Lusby, convinced that nothing was adding up about Katie Simpson's attempted suicide, had turned detective. From the minute he heard she had been brought to hospital having been found hanged in the house she shared with his half cousin Johnny Creswell and her sister Christina, along with their two children, he simply knew something was wrong.

Paul had first met Katie at his uncle Herbie's Donegal equestrian centre years before, when she was a young teenager, and since then he had watched her develop both on horseback and into a vibrant young woman. He could see how hard she worked and how little she got back and knew that Creswell was a hard task-master. Katie had sporadically confided in him about her predicament. When her sister Christina gave birth to her second child, six months before Katie's death, she told Paul that she was stuck for another seven years as a free babysitter for Creswell. Paul had spent a lot of time with the Simpson sisters and Creswell and they'd even socialised together, attending hunt balls and family events at Herbie Lusby's stately Port Hall. He'd heard Creswell make nasty remarks to the girls, but any time he tried to ask them about it they'd deny there was anything wrong and quickly change the subject. But Katie and suicide? Now, that was definitely something that didn't sit right with him. He couldn't think of anyone less likely to make an attempt on her own life. Katie had a positive outlook on life and was a problem-solver; and on top of that Paul was sure that there was a romance brewing between her and Shane McCloskey – and Katie had been glowing.

When he heard the news he'd first gone to Donna Creswell's house to ask about Johnny and Christina and how they were doing but had found her odd and unfriendly. She'd told him to call Christina's phone as Johnny's was switched off. The day after Katie was brought to hospital he visited the Gortnessy House and found a collection of people there, including Hayley Robb, who, he would later say, tried to cut him off at the front door in the hope that he wouldn't go in. Shane McCloskey was in the sitting room, but Paul later told friends he was very quiet and had nothing much to say. Hayley told Paul that Katie had been feeling low, which he found strange, and that Johnny and Christina were upstairs in bed, which he thought was even odder.

By 7 August Paul had become so suspicious about Katie's supposed suicide attempt that he made his first call to the anonymous Crimestoppers line saying that police should investigate and see if Johnny Creswell had anything to do with it. Unknown to him, others were uncomfortable with the scenario that was playing out at Altnagelvin Hospital, where, along with her close family, Creswell was one of those regularly at Katie's bedside.

As the days wore on and Katie continued to cling to life, Paul, like others who knew her, hoped that her fitness and her youth would be on her side and that she might survive, but when she passed away in the early hours of 10 August all hopes were dashed

and he made a second call to Crimestoppers with further information about Creswell and how he believed he operated like a sort
of cult leader with women at his command.

At the wake Paul watched Creswell and his bizarre behaviour
around Katie who was laid out in her coffin in a bedroom. He
saw him joke and walk forward with his hand extended when
mourners came to sympathise with her family. He heard him
whisper to one: 'How could Katie do this to me?' He heard about
the inappropriate remarks he'd made over her body and how he'd
joked that she'd never brushed her hair and was a 'dirty wee
bitch'. He saw him straining himself to cry and at the pub, after
her burial, he learned that Katie's phone was missing. When a
relative of Katie called him to a quiet corner to ask him what he
knew of Creswell's personality and what he could be capable of,
he realised that others also believed that Creswell could have had
something to do with her death. That night he was sure that Jill
Robinson was listening to his conversation and a deep feeling of
paranoia started to settle in. When Johnny arrived at the pub
where mourners had gathered he was jovial and loud, not at all
what Paul would expect from someone who'd had such a hands-on
and traumatic role in Katie's end. 'He seemed more preoccupied
getting himself registered for a showjumping event the next day
than mourning Katie,' he would later tell friends.

People in Derry had been talking about Katie Simpson, and
Paul discovered that medical staff had been concerned about
injuries she had presented with and with aspects of Creswell's
story that they found hard to believe. He picked up the phone
and called Crimestoppers again to fill in investigators and tell
them to treat Creswell like a 'cult leader' surrounded by supportive

women. He started to actively make his own enquiries about what had gone on and decided to focus on Katie's phone and why it could be missing. He couldn't understand how Katie had called in sick to work when she didn't have her mobile. He went up to Noel Kelly's yard, where Katie had been working in the run-up to her death. Kelly would later appear on the BBC's *Spotlight* and detail how shocked he was when he heard Katie had committed suicide. He described her as a dedicated and committed worker. It was two weeks after the funeral and Paul Lusby wanted to know if she'd made the call, but nobody could confirm that she had, and Kelly told him that Katie was so dedicated that if she was even two minutes late she'd be on the phone to tell him.

At the same time Paul offered to help Christina vacate the house at Gortnessy where Creswell said he'd found Katie hanging. As he cleaned he noticed blood on the frame of the door of the master bedroom, low down near the floor. At the same time Paul was trying to gain the trust of Shane McCloskey to find out what had gone on in the last days of Katie's life. He liked Shane and could see he was scared and found it odd that he was introducing himself as Katie's 'friend' when it was clear the pair had had a relationship. Shane eventually told Paul about their liaison on the Saturday night and about the messages and the fake ones he had sent her as she competed in the last show in Lurgan. And he showed him that last message, which a court would later hear the Crown believed Creswell had sent on Katie's phone. Months before a murder enquiry would ever be launched and while police were processing Katie's death as a suicide, Paul Lusby took one look at the message and said: 'That's him. There is no way Katie would write that.'

As Paul continued snooping around, Creswell got word that he was asking a lot of questions and phoned him three times, leaving him messages. Then he phoned a relation: 'Tell Paul I'll come up and see him sometime . . . I'll just surprise him.' The veiled threat terrified Paul but still he kept up his investigations, believing he was uncovering a murder. Convinced the police were working away in the background, and unaware that they were also stonewalling Tanya Fowles and others, Paul contacted Strand Road Station and eventually got a call from an officer, who agreed to meet him. Over hours he spilled out his suspicions and his findings from his unofficial investigation. He was convinced that Creswell would be arrested and that police were literally on his trail but instead they were not joining the dots and the detailed notes that the officer had taken about his suspicions and his civilian findings had been shredded.

Paul continued to try to probe into Creswell and the circle of women around him to try to understand their dynamic. He could see that they were strong and loyal, but the odd time the women could turn on one another. He also wondered why Creswell was anxious that Shane McCloskey not state he was in a relationship with Katie. Had Creswell sexually assaulted Katie and was his DNA on her body? Did he need people to think they were in a relationship?

Lusby was highly stressed and paranoid by the time the PSNI launched an official murder investigation into the death of Katie Simpson. Months after he first tried to raise the alarm, police had finally become suspicious about what had occurred. Lusby had danced a difficult waltz while he'd tried to find out what he could from the people who knew Katie. He had been friends with Johnny for a period of years but he was afraid of him too and was aware that he knew everything about him, including where he lived and who his relations were. He was also friends with Christina and knew their two little children, Sandra and Michael, who would be deprived of a father should police arrest Creswell. He felt a mixture of guilt and resolve to get to the bottom of things for Katie, who'd been silenced permanently in death. He became increasingly worried when he observed another young girl starting to spend more and more time in Creswell's company. Just 16, she looked like they all once had; Hayley, Christina, Katie and Rose. He placed posters on the roads around Derry calling for 'Justice for Katie' and he began to campaign for safeguarding of young girls in the horse industry.

When Creswell was arrested Lusby felt a sense of relief, but when he was granted bail he suspected that he still had a lot of support and that many still believed he was innocent. He felt a mix of emotions about Christina; while he couldn't comprehend how difficult it must have been for her that her partner had been accused of the murder and rape of her little sister, he suspected she was still in touch with Johnny. On the day he got bail the court had been told she'd furnished the prison with a new number she'd obtained in order to keep her distance from him. Christina had continued living with Creswell in the run-up to his arrest and he knew that the Crown was going to say that she'd seen him in bed with her sister the night before he faked her suicide. He wondered what it must have been like living with Creswell and what long-term effects that could have on her. He'd tried to help her salvage what she could of her stock and stay financially safe for her children, but he had become drawn in a long way out of a misplaced sense of guilt.

Lusby couldn't keep up with the dynamics of the women. It made his head spin. Christina told him that Hayley had caused a lot of problems because she had wanted Johnny all to herself; and she seemed to fall in and out with Jill Robinson. But the pressure on all of them was palpable as many people turned their backs on them, wanting nothing to do with the toxic Creswell. Lusby claimed that it had taken police a very long time to launch a murder investigation and that they had ignored his concerns. He'd made complaints to the Ombudsman, three in total, about the way he had been treated by police and the way they mishandled his information. His first two were rejected because he was not related to Katie, but he finally got one over the line when he said the notes taken by the officer should never have been destroyed. All the while Paul was trying to hold his own family together, but the mental pressure on him finally became too much. Tragically, in July 2022 he took his own life. Family members would later say he was a victim of Creswell and the evil that surrounded him.

Tanya Fowles could see Paul Lusby spiralling into mental turmoil as he tried to make sense of Creswell and the characters surrounding him. She'd hoped that he would seek help in the arms of his supportive family, whom he loved. Tanya had also been eaten up by Creswell and the shocking case of Katie Simpson, but the journalist had focused her frustrations on the PSNI who, she believed, should be held accountable for their inaction in the early months. The ripple effects of that had been hard to measure. Creswell had been empowered and had lived free for six months with time to bed down his story and to convince others to stick by him. When he was eventually charged he'd been able to get bail because the pathology report still stated hanging as a possible cause of death. CCTV that should have been harvested had been recorded over because the police were too slow, forensic opportunities had been missed and for months Creswell had had free access to people who could have been witnesses. His death by suicide after the first day of the trial had left more questions than answers. It had also meant the collapse of other cases against him; charges of sex with a minor, three separate historic sexual assaults against children, and physical assaults. And still more victims were coming forward all the time from all over Northern Ireland.

Pushing hard for the Ombudsman inquiry, Tanya had also focused on the other arms of the state, such as social services, which she believed had failed Katie – and others – and on the people who hadn't done their jobs properly. She had fired off questions, Freedom of Information requests and done whatever else she could, but she felt she was getting nowhere quick. She believed that an overarching public enquiry was needed to find out just how Creswell had almost got away with murder. That inquiry, she believed, should focus on the equestrian industry in which he had hidden in plain sight for years, with the support of many people who turned a blind eye to his twisted personality. 'There are so many victims out there. It's beyond shocking,' she texted me one evening. 'I've enquiries with multiple agencies seeking their support for an equivalent of Operation Yewtree, like [Jimmy] Savile. Creswell is dead but his victims need a voice and the equestrian industry needs to be investigated as closely as entertainment was by Yewtree.'

We meet at Castle Leslie, the place where Creswell brought Abi Lyle more than ten years before; where he strung her from a tree deep in the forest; where he sweated from the exertion of the beating he gave her; and where he could have killed her, just as he killed Katie. It's calm and elegant in the hotel and we order some lunch. More than six months ago Tanya sat in my car and showed me around her home town, where this terrible story played out and where a monster hid in plain sight. 'Do you see now how he was enabled?' she asked. Nuala Lappin has joined us too. Retired now from the PSNI, she has closely followed the case of Katie Simpson and the investigation into her death. She takes out her phone and shows me a picture of two identical young women with flowing hair and wide smiles. They look like sisters, twins almost, but they are Abi Lyle and Katie Simpson, snaps taken when they were the same age. 'He had a type,' she says.

There is so much to consider that it is hard to know where to start, but we finally settle on how easy it was for Creswell to operate within the equestrian industry, where many looked the other way as he made crude sexual remarks and beat and terrorised women in his company. According to Sarah, he did that quite openly at an Antrim yard, and that was long after he had served a sentence for beating Abi Lyle and threatening to throw her into a bath of bleach.

'We've been very focused on the PSNI and their errors and delays in launching a murder inquiry, but if we rewind further there is a very uncomfortable run-up to that and for years and years Creswell was able to frequently abuse young women while many in the equestrian industry looked the other way. There was a party thrown for him, for God's sake, when he got out of jail for Abi Lyle – a party for an abuser. And he went right back at it. He was empowered,' says Tanya.

On his release from prison Katie was just 10 years old and it was at that point, a court would later hear, that he had started to groom and abuse her. Creswell had begun a relationship with her sister Christina, who had stood by him during the court proceedings in the Abi case and presented herself as his partner, although she was only 15 years old. Jill Robinson, too, had his back and had even given a statement to his solicitor claiming that Abi had injured herself. On his release he went straight back to work and was even given a starring role on a Channel 4 advert for the Grand National. Creswell was seen as the wronged man, while his victim, Abi, who had bravely reported him to police, had felt so ostracised from the equestrian community in Northern Ireland that she had moved to Britain. Instead of learning from his experience he reverted to form almost immediately.

Abi Lyle was brave and ahead of her time. Her sister Rachel points out that there is a massive difference now in how the kind of abuse she suffered is handled.

I've been a barrister for 23 years and when I started domestic violence was kind of laughed at. Over the years people started to pay much more attention to it and at one time, during one of the big bail applications, a Senior for Creswell referenced what happened to Abi as 'domestic'. And I was really annoyed but Justice John O'Hara came straight in and said 'yes but he would have got a lot more for that now'.

Abi came out and did so much with Women's Aid and there were articles about her and she was so brave speaking out back then because it just wasn't done. And it's only in the last sort of 'me too era' you see people speaking out. And now we have this coercive control legislation but I still do cases where there is a massive disconnect with police officers on the ground, some will see the ongoing harassment, but many don't join the dots.

When Creswell took his own life, derailing his trial, Abi got the best news she could have ever wanted. Selected for the Olympic Games, at which she was set to ride her 13-year-old gelding Geraldo, affectionately known as Arty, she told *Horse and Hound* magazine:

When I moved to England in 2009, my ultimate goal was to do a Prix St George. So to say that the Olympics was beyond my wildest dreams is a teeny understatement. So many people have led me, propped me up, walked beside me and contributed in so many ways to get to this. There's so much to thank. But the first and most important thing to thank is Arty, you have no idea what you have done for me. I'll spend the rest of our lives making sure you feel like the most loved horse in the world and that you never ever want for anything.

Abi went on to compete in the games and proudly represent her country. Her respect for her horse was something that Creswell never showed. How many animals were broken or whipped or injured under his fury, and who is there to speak for them? They can never tell their story or reveal the fear they felt as they heard the footsteps approaching across a lonely stableyard.

Who knows what could have happened if Sarah's complaint had not been shelved in 2017 when the PSNI gave up trying to track a jockey whose race meetings were listed on point-to-point events? If they'd found him, would that have stopped him? Were proper efforts made to find him even when his own legal team admitted that he was working in Antrim every day as normal? That was only the beginning of the errors made by police and, as the leaked Ombudsman's report shows, a lack of an investigative mindset almost saw him get away with Katie's murder.

Nuala Lappin successfully investigated Creswell as a PSNI officer but she cannot understand what went wrong with procedures in 2020.

After I heard the circumstances of what happened; you know, this guy finds a girl hanging and allegedly cuts her down, tries CPR and then carries her into the car? I mean the very first thing there is you don't carry a dead weight. There is no way that happened like that. I've cut people down but there is no way I'd be able to carry them. Then I found out he got her into the front seat and was sitting upright. Excuse my French but that's bollocks. If he did take her to the car he didn't do it on his own. And how the police accepted that I will never know.

She tells me that she attended many sudden deaths during her career and the premise is that everything is treated suspiciously until it is proved otherwise.

Uniforms will attend but the fact is that they have the least experience. A sergeant is supposed to come out and they will bring CID in if necessary. I look at this and it is incomprehensible to me that Creswell's version of events is simply accepted. The whole thing is so odd and particularly the way she is transferred to the ambulance. Why did a police car not head straight away to Gortnessy and seal it off? Yet he is able to go back and ultimately have a shower and change his clothes. That is obscene. Everything is wrong and the living situation is bizarre by anybody's standards. There was a lack of investigative curiosity from the team the first time around but I think the second one missed things as well. To me, from the minute this started there was zero procedure, yet the PSNI lay this out for you as if you are two years old. And it doesn't matter that the family isn't shouting about it, in issues of domestic abuse you have to disempower the victim in a way so you can navigate the complexities of what is going on.

For Tanya it's the details of what happened in that house that still remain unsolved.

There is still no definitive position on what actually happened to Katie between leaving that showjumping event and being presented to paramedics on the side of the road by Jonathan Creswell. There are the accounts of those who were in her company in those last final hours, but the more I go through them the more I wonder what really happened and will we ever get the truth. So we have the CCTV and the cell site analysis which tells us where she was with Creswell until the early hours of August the third when they arrive back to Gortnessy Meadows, but there the real mystery begins.

When he was arrested Creswell told police that he and Katie had had sex on the bonnet of his car before returning home after midnight. The stories change and are fluid. Rose still maintains she talked to Katie when she came in, Christina sees him in bed with her at four-thirty a.m. and then he is in the spare room when she is leaving the house. Rose claims she brings her tea and chats with her at seven a.m. But Katie is all the while raped and assaulted by Creswell. She is alive when she comes home but she is unconscious and dying by eight a.m. When did that fatal attack occur and how did Creswell get Katie into the car? They are the real questions that remain and which should be still under investigation now.

Creswell told Hayley to call an ambulance and according to him lifted Katie up, taking her full weight with one arm while on the phone. He said she 'flopped' as he cut her down, that he started CPR and then struggled to hold her up and dragged her to the car. The front door wasn't covered by CCTV so this was never captured. He claimed Katie was blue and her tongue was 'green'. In the audio call with NIAS [Northern Ireland Ambulance Service] he states he put Katie in the rear of his car and set off, but she was in fact in the passenger seat of her own car. He'd said he cleared the rear seat and laid her down when they told him to when he was counting 'one, two, three, four' into the phone, but she was upright when they got there and the back seat held two child seats.

Katie weighed roughly eleven stone. Creswell was shorter than her and had an issue with his leg. He gave conflicting accounts of cutting Katie down and later claimed he unclipped the strap, which allowed her to fall onto the stairs. Later in a police interview he said he lifted her to get her head free from the noose. Whatever he did, I agree with Nuala and I believe he couldn't have done it alone. This is a dead weight, awkward and unable to assist in any way, but Creswell says he drags her along the hallway and out to her car. It may be possible but certainly very difficult and surely not all in the four-minute timescale he suggested.

Nuala is a straight talker. She joined the PSNI in 2002 and spent a few years in uniform before the Chief in Cookstown offered her a domestic abuse post. She hadn't particularly wanted the role but it was nine-to-five and as a single parent with a young child, it brought stability. 'When I decided to do it I knew I would do it as best I could. I went in and the first thing I did was look at the worst offenders in the district and those were the guys I targeted. I was getting intelligence from uniforms about them, about new partners, and I became their stalker.' She had settled into her new role and had become well versed in the complexities of domestic violence by the time Abi Lyle appeared on the scene.

Abi came onto my radar because some of what happened to her had happened in Bangor. I had dealt with her family and they had voiced their concerns. I made contact with Abi eventually and she was very resistant, very controlled and making excuses for him. And then came the day when she rang in to the office and it was by pure luck she got me there. She screamed down the phone that he had kidnapped her and she was at his house. I didn't even know where Caledon was, but I just hopped in the car and drove . . . so I got there and pulled up to the back door and it opened very quickly and he came charging out. I was in plain clothes and held up the warrant card and he was roaring and shouting and telling me to fuck off. I had to push him back. He was in my face. I could see her cowering behind him and I just ordered her to get into my car. He puffed up his chest and squared up to me . . . and because of that I had him arrested. The difference in him the next day was incredible. He was sitting back and he really fancied himself. He told me that I fancied him and that all women did! He was so arrogant. I was used to dealing with the highly explosive male but with him it wasn't like that. I let him talk and it was all 'woe is me' and 'Abi is a psycho.' I was doing the empathy thing and he is saying to me, 'you know how women can't control themselves'. He couldn't stop talking. It was insane. When I started challenging him, then it changed. He got tetchy. At one point he pretended to hyperventilate. I have never met anyone more arrogant in all my days. He was brimming with confidence.

While Nuala and her team had got the better of Creswell, she also got an insight into the women that surrounded him. She had taken a call one day from Jill Robinson demanding that she take a statement from her about Abi Lyle. She saw her attend court along with Christina and support him throughout.

Tanya is frustrated by the police attitude to the women who surrounded Creswell, some of whom have been deemed his victims. 'All of them said that Katie was in a very dark place. That was pumped relentlessly at the wake and the funeral. Yet she wasn't in any dark place and they knew he had beaten her. Yes, the second investigation team went after Creswell but in my mind he never worked alone. He had a team around him who facilitated him and from day one Johnny was in charge. It was only that Hayley Robb came in and volunteered the information about the cover-up that any of the women were prosecuted at all.'

Creswell ultimately got bail on the murder charge because the case against him was circumstantial. Opportunities missed by the original investigation team read like an incredible drama about incompetent policing, and still nothing about Katie's death adds up.

Many who stood at her graveside and watched Creswell lower her coffin into the ground believed they were in a dream. 'Speaking for myself and others that were there, we watched that funeral in the hopes that the blue lights were coming, but nothing happened. That was a double blow, to sit and watch this man enter stage left and act out a devotion to this girl we knew he had killed. You didn't need to be Sherlock Holmes to work it out,' says Tanya. 'He'd been at her bedside as she breathed her last breath. No doubt those around her were in a distressed state but he had the audacity to stand with them, to be at her side until the end.'

Ironically for the PSNI there was an absolute failure to learn from the recommendations and the outrage over the case of Hazel Buchanan and dentist Colin Howell, a prisoner who was on his way into Maghaberry Prison as Creswell was walking out. Together Buchanan and Howell staged the double 'suicide' of their partners Trevor Buchanan and Lesley Howell in a scene which the Ombudsman later found so crass that it was fanciful, yet police believed the story they were told by the murderers. The report found that the flawed investigation had lacked objectivity and that police had accepted the accounts of what had happened from killers Howell and Buchanan, despite the fact that they were both shown to be liars from early on. Police Ombudsman Al Hutchinson said the investigation missed evidential opportunities and he found that 'There was a very early assumption of suicide. I have seen little evidence that this assumption was subject to any test or challenge by the investigators . . . Evidential opportunities were overlooked or ignored, lines of enquiry were not fully explored and police did not consider the inconsistencies and discrepancies in the evidence which began to emerge.' Among the criticisms listed, it was noted that the scene had not been dealt with properly and forensic opportunities had been missed. The Ombudsman found that police accepted Howell's account of how injuries to Trevor Buchanan's face, not consistent with the suicide scenario, may have happened, and made no further inquiries about them, despite concerns raised by at least two people at his funeral. 'Police continued to show an investigative bias and adhere to the suicide theory, despite the fact that the two main people promoting it, Howell and Buchanan, had lied to them,' said the Police Ombudsman. The story was the stuff of dinner party discussion and would later be turned into a TV drama, but at the heart of it lay massive failings in a police investigation which the public were assured would never happen again. In its statement the PSNI said it accepted the findings: 'The PSNI will conduct a review of its current procedures to ensure that sudden deaths are subject to thorough investigation.'

But years later a hauntingly familiar scenario played out. For Tanya, there is still far more to unravel about the world of Creswell and his followers.

When Katie was murdered Creswell was living with Christina, their children, Katie and Rose and in a relationship with Hayley. As the murder case crawled through the justice system, more women were coming forward reporting similar abuse. Some spoke out while Creswell was briefly remanded in custody, such was their fear of reprisals. An obvious equation is whether or not the role of sectors of the equestrian industry was similar to what happened with Jimmy Savile in the entertainment industry. The comparisons are stark. After Savile's death and without a single charge being brought against him Operation Yewtree uncovered a whole web of abuse, facilitation and cover-up. Following Creswell's death further people have come forward with similar harrowing and disturbing concerns. They will never see him prosecuted but instead there are many yet to speak out who are victims and there is a sport which they say views abuse as something to be unfettered.

Did Creswell work alone? Were others of a similar persuasion drawn to him? What of Aaron McWilliams, the young man who'd befriended Creswell during summer trips to his grandmother near Tynan, when he earned pocket money as a babysitter? Years later he was convicted of sexually assaulting a four-year-old child and after serving his sentence was released early on licence, but went on to commit the same crime against another child of the same age. During that investigation in 2017 his phone was seized and detectives found almost 2,500 images of children plus an extensive collection of videos he'd made of himself abusing his young victims. The prolific child predator would be interviewed about the material as he languished in prison. Twenty-four victims aged between four and 14 years old were identified, some of whom had been in Ireland when the offences occurred.

Nuala Lappin believes Creswell took on a role as the 'father' of his household, with Christina at his side. 'It is all a bit cultish if you ask me. A lot of people are afraid of him but there are a lot who are obsessed with him. Jill Robinson has a relationship with him and they break up and she moves on but she is still obsessed and still there loyal to the end. Christina is in a relationship with him to the extent that they have two children, but he is with other women very openly and she seems to accept that. There is a dynamic when a woman is with an abusive partner that, to outsiders, she makes it look safe. All the women make him look safe when you are looking in. But they are all being abused and controlled,' she says.

Both Nuala and Tanya agree that of all those who supported Creswell and hid his crimes, Hayley Robb was the most honest and forthcoming. 'She ultimately makes sense of it all. When she comes forward, which is after Creswell is already charged, she gives a narrative that explains it. Had the trial continued she would have blown it all open,' says Nuala.

I think she has shown a level of vulnerability. She has felt accountable and I genuinely do think that. She has come and broken down and told them this awful story, the most humiliating details of her life; that she is having sex with a guy who is using her and whose partner is aware. In domestic violence relationships people know they have to leave, they don't need you to scream it at them. They feel like a piece of shit but they often can't find a way to face up to it. In Hayley's case, her conscience brought her to the police. She would have won that case for the police. It was very circumstantial and you have Hayley coming in offering first person witness. It changed the whole thing.

Was it Hayley who Creswell blamed in his as-yet unpublished suicide note found near his body at his bail address? Or was it simply the weight of the evidence against him? Tanya says she watched Creswell physically crumble during the opening day of his trial.

Of course none of it would have been a shock. He would have known what was coming from the book of evidence, but the trial had been delayed so much as they were getting all the expert reports which had come in one by one. There was delay, delay, delay and he was out on bail getting on with things. Then the jury was picked and that took the guts of a day as he rejected one after another; he was wanting more women and at one stage it was six and six until eventually it ended up with eight women and four men. A dangerous tactic, some would say. As the jury was sworn in, the court was told the defence wouldn't be calling one witness. Not one. When I heard that I knew the case was over. You could see how tense Creswell was. The next day when the case opened I watched him as we got this sort of condensed trial. I have never seen an opening like it. I kept waiting for his counsel to jump up and complain but they didn't. They went through the text messages, the camera footage from the hospital and the witnesses that would be called. I could see him going down and down and he actually nearly went foetal at one point. It was like he wanted to put his fingers in his ears. You have to remember that Hayley has pleaded guilty and that Jill and Rose have pleaded too after that. So he is goosed. He went home that night and he knew it. His house of cards had fallen.

Inquests into the deaths of Jonathan Creswell and Katie Simpson are due to be held at some point in the future.

ACKNOWLEDGEMENTS

There is a huge darkness to the story of Katie Simpson, a young woman taken in the prime of her life by a predator who almost got away with murder. Many people failed Katie in her life and in her death, yet there were some who were there for her and who have fought hard for justice and to shine a light into the murky world in which she existed. Some knew her and were kind but others are strangers, ordinary people who did their jobs well and those who spoke out despite the fallout. Creswell's brave victim Abi Lyle, former domestic violence officer Nuala Lappin and those like Paul Lusby – who tried to do something in the face of huge resistance – restore our faith in people and their morals.

Hayley Robb did wrong but in finally telling the truth she blew the whistle on Creswell's world of secrets, violence and coercion. She should be recognised for that.

And finally, while she would hate to be described as a hero, journalist Tanya Fowles surely stands out for her tenacity, her professionalism and her humanity. That demonstrates her admirable principles and beliefs in right and wrong.

I would like to thank many people for their help as I journeyed into Katie's world; most importantly Tanya for all the work she did on this story and exposing the failures of people and institutions.

To Nicole Moran of Madden & Finucane Solicitors for her excellent legal read. To Ciaran Sheils for the guided tours of Derry and its surrounds and all the history lessons. And as always, to Deirdre Nolan, Publishing Director of Eriu, Bonnier Books and Lisa Gilmour, Assistant Editor.